Success in Math

Basic Algebra

Student Edition

GLOBE FEARON

Pearson Learning Group

Executive Editor: Barbara Levadi
Market Manager: Sandra Hutchison
Senior Editor: Francie Holder
Editors: Karen Bernhaut, Douglas Falk, Amy Jolin
Editorial Assistant: Kris Shepos-Salvatore
Editorial Consultant: Harriet Slonim
Production Manager: Penny Gibson
Production Editor: Walt Niedner
Interior Design: The Wheetley Company
Electronic Page Production: The Wheetley Company
Cover Design: Pat Smythe

ISBN 0-8359-1188-8
Printed in the United States of America
9 10   05 04

1-800-321-3106
www.pearsonlearning.com

Contents

Chapter 1

The Language of Algebra

OBJECTIVES:

In this chapter, you will learn

- *To use variables to represent numbers*
- *To express numbers in exponential form*
- *To understand and use grouping symbols*
- *To understand the order of operations*
- *To understand and use inverse operations*
- *To translate between verbal expressions and algebraic expressions*

People use language to communicate with each other. English is the language most commonly spoken in the United States. There are at least fifteen other languages, each of which is spoken by more than 100,000 Americans.

All languages have at least two things in common. First, they let words stand for objects and ideas. Second, they have rules that tell speakers how to put words together.

Top 10 Non-English Languages Spoken at Home by Americans (1990 Census)	
Language	**Number of Speakers**
Spanish	17,339,000
French	1,703,000
German	1,547,000
Italian	1,309,000
Chinese	1,249,000
Tagalog	843,000
Polish	723,000
Korean	626,000
Vietnamese	507,000
Portugese	430,000

	English	Spanish	French	German	Italian
	dog	perro	chien	Hund	cane
	pencil	lapiz	crayon	Bleistift	lapis

This chapter is called "The Language of Algebra" because algebra, like all mathematics, is a kind of language.

◄ 1•1 Understanding Variables and Expressions

▌IN THIS LESSON, YOU WILL LEARN
To use variables to represent unknown quantities

WORDS TO LEARN
Variables *letters used to represent one or more numbers*

Variable expressions *expressions that include variables, numbers, and mathematical symbols*

Evaluate *find the value of an expression*

Donna works Saturdays as a cashier in a restaurant. Every Saturday $9 in taxes is deducted, or subtracted, from her pay. How can Donna write a variable expression to show the amount left after deductions?

New Idea

Letters used to represent, or stand for, numbers are **variables** (VAIR-e-uh-buhlz). **Variable expressions** (VAIR-ee-uh-buhl ehks-PREHSH-uhnz) contain numbers, variables, and signs for adding, subtracting, multiplying, or dividing.

Here are some variable expressions:

$$3 + x \qquad\qquad \frac{t}{7} \qquad\qquad 15 \bullet n \qquad\qquad 32x$$

To show multiplication in algebra, instead of the multiplication symbol, $\times$, we use a raised dot, "$\bullet$", as in $3 \bullet n$. Or we write $3n$, or use parentheses as in $(3)(n)$.

Donna has $9 deducted from her paycheck. If p stands for Donna's pay, then $p - 9$ is a variable expression for the amount left. To **evaluate** (ee-VAL-yoo-ayt) a variable expression, we replace the variable with a number.

Example: Evaluate the variable expression $p - 9$ if p is $72.

$$p = 72$$
$$p - 9 = 72 - 9 \qquad \leftarrow \text{Subtract 9 from both sides of}$$
$$p - 9 = 63 \qquad\qquad\quad \text{the equation.}$$

Donna has $63 left after deductions.

Now suppose Donna gets a $45 bonus, so $45 is added to her pay. The variable expression $p + 45$ shows this.

Example: Evaluate the variable expression $p + 45$ if p is $63.

$$p = 63$$
$$p + 45 = 63 + 45 \qquad \leftarrow \text{Add 45 to both sides of the}$$
$$p + 45 = 108 \qquad\qquad\quad \text{equation.}$$

Donna's pay after her bonus is $108.

In these examples, p had two different values. In fact, a variable can have many different values.

✓**Check the Math**

1. **a.** Evaluate the expression $150 \cdot n$ for $n = 12$. _____

   b. Does $150n$ have the same value? Explain.

   _____

▸**Focus on the Idea**

A variable represents a number. A variable expression may contain numbers, variables, and operation signs such as $+$, $-$, $\bullet$, or $\div$. To evaluate a variable expression, replace the variable with a number.

Practice

Evaluate each variable expression. The first one is done for you.

2. $m + 8$ for $m = 5$
   $5 + 8 = 13$

3. $w - 4$ for $w = 12$
   _____

4. $5 \bullet p$ for $p = 7$
   _____

5. $h \div 2$ for $h = 30$
   _____

6. $6 \bullet e + 5$ for $e = 3$
   _____

7. $\frac{c}{9} - 4$ for $c = 45$
   _____

8. $2r + 120$ for $r = 5$
   _____

9. $4ac$ for $a = 3$, $c = \frac{1}{4}$
   _____

10. $2s - 8 + \frac{s}{4}$ for $s = 12$
    _____

Apply the Idea

11. Reread the problem at the beginning of the lesson. Suppose Donna works h hours and earns $6 each hour.

    a. Is $6h - 9$ an expression for Donna's pay? Explain.

    _____

    b. If h stands for 6.25 hours, how much will Donna earn after deductions? _____

✏ **Write About It**

12. Describe the difference between a variable and a variable expression.

    _____

    _____

A manufacturer makes boxes that are 8 inches long, 8 inches wide, and 8 inches high. Find the volume of a box, or the number of cubic units needed to fill it, by multiplying its length times its width times its height. Each box has a volume of 8 inches • 8 inches • 8 inches, or 512 cubic inches. What is a shorter way to write 8 • 8 • 8?

New Idea

You can use a base and an exponent to write the product of a number multiplied by itself.

The **base** (bays) is the number that is multiplied by itself. The **exponent** (EHKS-pohn-uhnt) tells the number of times the base is multiplied. In the expression at the right, 8 is the base and 3 is the exponent. Read 8^3 as "8 to the third power." A number whose value is expressed as a base and exponent is written in **exponential form** (ehks-poh-NEHN-shuhl fawrm).

$$\overset{\text{exponent}}{\underset{\text{base}}{8 \cdot 8 \cdot 8 = 8^3}}$$

A number raised to the first power equals the number itself. So 6^1 equals 6. A number raised to the second or third power is read in a special way. Read 15^2 as "fifteen squared." Read 7^3 as "seven cubed."

Examples: Express 14^3 another way.

$$14^3 = 14 \cdot 14 \cdot 14$$

Write $7 \cdot 7 \cdot 7 \cdot 7$ in exponential form.

$$7 \cdot 7 \cdot 7 \cdot 7 = 7^4$$

✓Check the Math

1. How can you express 2^4 as a product? _____

Focus on the Idea

To write the product of a number multiplied by itself several times, use a base and an exponent.

Practice

Write each expression in exponential form. Use a base and an exponent to write each product. Do not perform the multiplication. The first one is done for you.

2. $7 \cdot 7$

$\underline{7 \cdot 7 = 7^2}$

3. $6 \cdot 6 \cdot 6 \cdot 6$

$\underline{\hspace{3cm}}$

4. $9 \cdot 9 \cdot 9 \cdot 9 \cdot 9 \cdot 9$

$\underline{\hspace{3cm}}$

5. $12 \cdot 12 \cdot 12$

$\underline{\hspace{3cm}}$

6. $2 \cdot 2 \cdot 2 \cdot 2 \cdot 2 \cdot 2 \cdot 2$

$\underline{\hspace{3cm}}$

7. $8.5 \cdot 8.5$

$\underline{\hspace{3cm}}$

Express each value as a product. The first one is done for you.

8. 4^3

$\underline{4 \cdot 4 \cdot 4}$

9. 10^2

$\underline{\hspace{3cm}}$

10. 25^3

$\underline{\hspace{3cm}}$

11. 3^6

$\underline{\hspace{3cm}}$

12. 2^5

$\underline{\hspace{3cm}}$

13. 97^1

$\underline{\hspace{3cm}}$

14. 3^4

$\underline{\hspace{3cm}}$

15. 6 to the third power

$\underline{\hspace{3cm}}$

16. 4.5 squared

$\underline{\hspace{3cm}}$

Evaluate each expression for $x = 3$.

17. x^4

$\underline{\hspace{4cm}}$

18. $x^2 + 2x$

$\underline{\hspace{4cm}}$

Apply the Idea

19. Your 2 parents and your $2 \cdot 2$, or 2^2, grandparents form the two generations before you. Write the number of ancestors that came 13 generations before you in exponential form.

$\underline{\hspace{12cm}}$

Write About It

20. Think about what you have learned about exponents.

a. Evaluate each of the following: 10^2, 10^3, 10^4, and 10^5.

$\underline{\hspace{12cm}}$

b. Write a rule to find the value of a number when 10 is the base and the exponent is any whole number.

$\underline{\hspace{12cm}}$

$\underline{\hspace{12cm}}$

◄1•3 Using Grouping Symbols

IN THIS LESSON, YOU WILL LEARN
To understand and use grouping symbols

WORDS TO LEARN
Parentheses *a grouping symbol*
Brackets *another grouping symbol*
Vinculum *a grouping symbol used to show division*

A symbol that you have used for many years, "−", the bar used in fractions, is a grouping symbol. It was first used by a mathematician named al-Hassar about the year 1050. It is called a vinculum and is only one of the grouping symbols used in algebra.

New Idea

Often, an expression must be treated as a single group. One way to group is to use **parentheses** (puh-REHN-thuh-seez), ( ). Numbers and variables grouped within parentheses may then be grouped within **brackets** (BRAK-ihts), [ ]. Still another way to group is to use the **vinculum** (VIHNG-kyuh-luhm), a grouping symbol used to show division.

To evaluate an expression, find the value of the numbers and variables within grouping symbols first. To evaluate an expression with a vinculum, do the work above and below the bar before dividing.

Example: Evaluate each expression.

$$3 + (4 \cdot 5) = 3 + 20 \qquad 5[(4 \cdot \tfrac{1}{2}) + 8] = 5[2 + 8]$$
$$= 23 \qquad\qquad\qquad\qquad = 5[10]$$
$$= 50$$

✓Check the Math

1. What is the difference between $(44 − 4) \cdot 4 \cdot 2$ and $44 − (4 \cdot 4 \cdot 2)$? Be sure to simplify the numbers within the parentheses first.

◄Focus on the Idea
Use parentheses and brackets to group the numbers or variables within an expression.

Practice

Write the numbers or variables in the expression whose value should be found first. The first two are done for you.

2. $(5 + 3) \div 4$

$\underline{\hspace{1em} 5 + 3 \hspace{1em}}$

3. $7 + (3 + 4) - 5$

$\underline{\hspace{1em} 3 + 4 \hspace{1em}}$

4. $24 + (600 + 10)$

$\underline{\hspace{3em}}$

5. $14 - (a + b)$

$\underline{\hspace{3em}}$

6. $t \cdot (n + 12)$

$\underline{\hspace{3em}}$

7. $(16 - 9) \div 5$

$\underline{\hspace{3em}}$

Find the value of each expression. The first one is done for you.

8. a. $18 - (5 \cdot 3)$ $\underline{18 - 15 = 3}$

b. $(18 - 5) \cdot 3$ $\underline{13 \cdot 3 = 39}$

9. a. $(25 + 5) \div 5$ $\underline{\hspace{3em}}$

b. $25 + (5 \div 5)$ $\underline{\hspace{3em}}$

10. $[12 - (3 + 8)]$ $\underline{\hspace{3em}}$

11. $(9 + 2) \cdot (9 - 2)$ $\underline{\hspace{3em}}$

12. $\frac{15 - 10}{4^2 - 8}$ $\underline{\hspace{3em}}$

13. $8 + (5 - 2)^5$ $\underline{\hspace{3em}}$

Evaluate each expression.

14. $a + (b \div c)$ for $a = 13$, $b = 21$, and $c = 7$ $\underline{\hspace{3em}}$

15. $(n^2 - p) \cdot 2$ for $n = 5$ and $p = 15$ $\underline{\hspace{3em}}$

Apply the Idea

16. Put parentheses and brackets in the following expression so that the resulting expression equals 30. $5 + 5 \div 5 \cdot 5$

$\underline{\hspace{30em}}$

17. Insert operation signs and grouping symbols to find the smallest whole number possible using the digits 2, 4, and 6.

$\underline{\hspace{30em}}$

18. Janice bought four CDs at $15 each and six tapes at $12 each. Use parentheses to write an expression that represents her total cost. Then find the total cost.

$\underline{\hspace{30em}}$

Write About It

19. Explain why we sometimes use more than one pair of grouping symbols in an expression.

$\underline{\hspace{30em}}$

$\underline{\hspace{30em}}$

$\underline{\hspace{30em}}$

1•4 Understanding Order of Operations

◄ **IN THIS LESSON, YOU WILL LEARN**

To understand the order in which mathematical operations are performed

WORDS TO LEARN

Mathematical operations *addition, subtraction, multiplication, or division of numbers and variables*

Mr. Garcia and his two children, both under 12, attend a movie. The expression $8 + 2 \cdot 5$ stands for the cost of the tickets.

Which is the correct way to find the cost?

Movie Tickets	
Adults:	$8
Children under 12:	$5

a. Add first and then multiply.
$8 + 2 = 10$ and $10 \cdot 5 = 50$; Cost: $50

b. Multiply first and then add.
$2 \cdot 5 = 10$ and $8 + 10 = 18$; Cost: $18

New Idea

Addition, subtraction, multiplication, and division are **mathematical operations** (math-uh-MAT-ih-kawl ahp-uhr-AY-shuhnz) performed on numbers and variables. The order in which you carry out operations as you simplify is important. It must be done in a certain order for your answer to be correct.

Order of Operations

First, do all calculations within parentheses, then brackets.
Second, do all calculations involving exponents.
Third, multiply or divide in order, from left to right.
Fourth, add or subtract in order, from left to right.

Examples: Evaluate. $5 + 2 \cdot 3$

$$5 + 2 \cdot 3 = 5 + 6 \qquad \leftarrow \text{Multiply. Then add.}$$

$$= 11$$

Evaluate. $4 \cdot (7 - 1)^2$

$$4 \cdot (7 - 1)^2 = 4 \cdot (6)^2 \quad \leftarrow \text{Work within parentheses.}$$
$$\text{Work with exponents.}$$

$$= 4 \cdot 36 \quad \leftarrow \text{Then multiply.}$$

$$= 144$$

Focus on the Idea

To evaluate an expression containing more than one operation, follow the rules for order of operations.

Practice

Indicate the operation you should perform first. The first one is done for you.

1. $6 + 8 \div 2$ ___÷ or divide___

2. $15 - 5 \cdot 2$ _____

3. $16 \div (2 + 6)^4$ _____

4. $3 \cdot 2^4$ _____

5. $30 \div 4 \cdot 2$ _____

6. $9 + 7 - 3 \cdot 4^3$ _____

Evaluate each expression. The first one is done for you.

7. $4 + 3 \cdot 2$ ___$4 + 6 = 10$___

8. $14 \div 2 - 2$ _____

9. $12 \cdot (5 - 3)$ _____

10. $(3 + 4)^2$ _____

11. $21 - 14 \div 7$ _____

12. $6 \cdot [4 + 3]$ _____

13. $(3 + 2)^2 \div 5$ _____

14. $6^2 \div 9 \div 2$ _____

15. $50 \div (2 + 8) \cdot 3$ _____

16. $7[16 \div (5 - 3)^3] + 1$ _____

Insert one pair of parentheses to make the expression true.

17. $2 + 5 \cdot 2 = 14$ _____

18. $20 \div 15 \div 3 = 4$ _____

19. $12 + 20 \div 4 - 5 = 3$ _____

20. $14 - 5 - 2 \cdot 2 = 14$ _____

Apply the Idea

21. Marcus earns $6 per hour. On Friday he works for 4 hours, and on Saturday he works for 7 hours. Each day he spends $3 on dinner. Write an expression for his earnings after he pays for two dinners. Find his earnings for the two days.

_____

Write About It

22. Use your calculator to evaluate this expression. $7 + 3 \cdot 2$ Does your calculator follow the rules for order of operations? Explain how you know.

_____

_____

◀**1•5** Using Inverse Operations

◀**IN THIS LESSON, YOU WILL LEARN**

To understand and use inverse operations

WORDS TO LEARN

Inverse operations *operations that reverse the results of other operations*

Keiko is the manager for a taxi company. She orders snow tires for the taxis. To determine the number of tires to buy, she multiplies the number of taxis by 4. If you know the number of tires she orders, how can you find the number of taxis the company owns?

New Idea

Each day we do many things and then reverse, or "undo," these same things. For example, we put on a coat and reverse that by taking off the coat. In mathematics, each arithmetic operation undoes another operation.

Adding undoes subtracting. Subtracting undoes adding. So, adding and subtracting are **inverse operations** (ihn-VERS ahp-uhr-AY-shuhnz).

Multiplying undoes dividing. Dividing undoes multiplying. So, multiplying and dividing are inverse operations.

We use inverse operations to solve problems. In the snow tire problem, Keiko multiplied the number of taxis by 4 to find the number of tires to order. If Keiko ordered 80 tires, you can find the number of taxis by dividing 80 by 4.

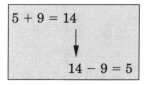

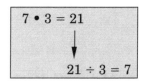

◀Focus on the Idea

Adding and subtracting "undo" each other. Multiplying and dividing "undo" each other. To undo an operation, apply its inverse operation.

Practice

Name the given operation. Then, name its inverse operation. The first one is done for you.

1. $8 - 6 = 2$

    _____subtraction_____

    _____addition_____

2. $14 \div 2 = 7$

    _____

    _____

3. $9 \cdot 3 = 27$

_____

_____

4. $13 + 8 = 21$

_____

_____

Name the inverse operation or operations.

5. $n \cdot 3$

_____

6. $n + 16$

_____

7. $n \div 12$

_____

8. $n - 35$

_____

9. $n - 3.5 \div 5$

_____

10. $n + 38.7 \cdot 67.5$

_____

Apply the Idea

11. The taxi company bought more taxis. The following year Keiko ordered 120 tires for all taxis.

    a. How many taxis does the company have? _____

    b. How can you be sure your answer is correct?

_____

_____

Write About It

12. Six friends went to a restaurant for dinner. The total bill came to $75.60, including tax and a tip. They decided that they would each pay $12.60.

    a. Explain how the friends determined how much each would pay.

_____

_____

_____

    b. Did the friends use inverse operations? If so, which operations were used?

_____

_____

⬇**1•6** Verbal Expressions and Algebraic Expressions

⬇**IN THIS LESSON, YOU WILL LEARN**

To translate between verbal expressions and algebraic expressions

WORDS TO LEARN

Algebraic symbols *another term for mathematical symbols*

Jeff is a painting contractor. He buys m gallons of white paint for $9 a gallon from a distributor. He also buys n tubes of colored paints to mix with the white paint. Each tube costs $3. Which expression represents the total amount he spends on paint?

$9 \bullet m \bullet 3 \bullet n$ $9 \bullet m + 3 \bullet n$ $9 + 3 \, (m \bullet n)$ $9 \bullet (m + 3 \bullet n)$

New Idea

Algebra is a language of symbols. To understand the language of algebra, you must be able to translate words into the correct symbols. You already know mathematical symbols, or **algebraic symbols** (al-juh-BRAY-ihk SIHM-buhls).

Here are some phrases that describe the mathematical operations.

Mathematical Operation	Word Expression	Variable Expression
addition	6 more than a number	$n + 6$
+	the sum of a number and 8	$n + 8$ or $8 + n$
	12 increased by a number	$12 + n$
subtraction	34 less than a number	$n - 34$
−	the difference between a number and 23	$n - 23$
	44 decreased by a number	$44 - n$
multiplication	the product of 4 and a number	$4 \bullet n$, $4n$, or $(4)(n)$
• or ( )	twice or double the number	$2 \bullet n$, $2n$, or $(2)(n)$
division	a number divided by 17	$n \div 17$
÷	the quotient of a number and 35	$n \div 35$

To express the amount that Jeff spends on paint in algebraic terms, think: The total amount he spends is the amount he spends on white paint plus the amount he spends on colored paint.

Think:

cost per gallon × number of gallons + cost per tube × number of tubes
(9 • m) + (3 • n)

⬛ Focus on the Idea

To write an expression in algebraic terms, translate words into numbers, variables, and symbols.

Practice

Write the symbol that represents the word. The first one is done for you.

1. product

  • or ( )

2. quotient

_____

3. difference

_____

Translate the phrase into an algebraic expression. Use a number, a variable, and an operation symbol. The first one is done for you.

4. six less than k

  $k - 6$

5. p divided by 2

_____

6. the sum of a and 3

_____

7. Cathy has d dollars. Write an algebraic expression for "the number of dollars Cathy has split five ways."

_____

8. Yolanda scored y points. Write an algebraic expression for "double the number of points Yolanda scored."

_____

Apply the Idea

9. There are x sandwiches on one tray and y sandwiches on another tray. Write an algebraic expression for the number of sandwiches each person will get if 5 people share all of them.

_____

✏ Write About It

10. Write a problem that can be expressed by this algebraic expression: $8 \cdot (a - b)$.

_____

_____

_____

Chapter 1   Review

In This Chapter, You Have Learned
- To use variables to represent numbers
- To understand and use exponents
- To understand and use parentheses and brackets
- To understand the order of operations
- To understand and use inverse operations
- To translate between verbal and algebraic expressions

Words You Know

From the lists of "Words to Learn," choose the word or phrase that best completes each statement.

1. A letter used to represent one or more numbers is a(n)

   _____.

2. You _____ a variable expression by replacing the variable with a number.

3. A(n) _____ tells the number of times a base is multiplied by itself.

4. The grouping symbols used in algebra are called

   _____, _____, and _____.

More Practice

Evaluate the variable expression.

5. $p \div 4$ for $p = 28$ _____

6. $a - 5$ for $a = 8$ _____

Use a base and an exponent to write each product. Do not perform the multiplication.

7. $7 \cdot 7 \cdot 7$ _____

8. $b \cdot b \cdot b \cdot b \cdot b$ _____

Write each expression as a product. Do not perform the multiplication.

9. 12^4 _____

10. d^2 _____

Evaluate.

11. 2^4 _____

12. 10^3 _____

13. 5^4 _____

14. 9.6^1 _____

15. $[18 - (14 + 4)]$ _____

16. $3 \cdot (2^3 - 6)$ _____

17. $6 + 2 \cdot 5$ _____

18. $30 \div 5 - 3$ _____

19. $(8 - 2)^2 \div 9$ _____

20. $32 - [(3 + 1)^2 - 2]$ _____

Name the operation that is the inverse of the one shown.

21. $18 \div 6$ _____

22. $24 - 5$ _____

Let _n_ represent a number. Write a variable expression.

23. a number minus 2 _____

24. k less than a number _____

25. the sum of 15 and half of a number _____

Problems You Can Solve

26. Paula lives m miles from her job. Write an expression for "8 miles farther than the distance Paula lives from her job."

    _____

27. Marco ordered n computers for his department. Write an expression for "7 less than double the number of computers Marco ordered."

    _____

28. **For Your Portfolio** Symbols play an important part in everyday life. Choose an activity of interest to you such as one that involves sports, school, or employment. Describe the activity. Give examples of symbols that are used in the activity. Explain how the symbols are used to make the activity easier for those who participate in it.

    _____

    _____

Chapter 1   Practice Test

Evaluate each expression for $a = 3$ and $b = 2$.

1. $b + 12$ _____

2. $5 \cdot a$ _____

3. $6 \cdot (a + b)$ _____

4. a^2 _____

5. $a + b$ _____

6. $a^2 + b^2$ _____

7. Write $h \cdot h \cdot h$ using a base and an exponent. _____

Evaluate each expression.

8. 3^4 _____

9. 12^2 _____

10. $24 \div (6 \div 2)$ _____

11. $m \cdot (4 + m)$ for $m = 3$ _____

12. $12 - 10 \div 2$ _____

13. $20 - 15 + 2$ _____

14. $14 \cdot (9 - 7)$ _____

15. $7 + (8 - 3)^2$ _____

Name the operation that is the inverse of the one shown.

16. $8 \div 2 = 4$ _____

17. 9 less than a number _____

18. 8 divided by a number _____

Write an expression.

19. Arnold's Restaurant had c customers on Tuesday. Write an expression for "8 less than 3 times the number of customers in the restaurant on Tuesday." _____

20. Ruby earned d dollars an hour as a department store sales clerk. After 6 months on the job, she received a raise of $1.25 per hour. Write an expression for her hourly wage after the raise. _____

Chapter 2

The Rules of Algebra

◢ OBJECTIVES:

In this chapter, you will learn

- *To recognize the difference between like terms and unlike terms*
- *To identify and use number properties*
- *To identify and use the Distributive Property of Multiplication Over Addition*
- *To simplify algebraic expressions by adding, subtracting, multiplying, or dividing like terms*

People involved in different occupations may use different units of measure. However, work with any measurements requires that the measurements be expressed in the same units. A storekeeper cannot add dimes and quarters, but she can add cents. A surveyor cannot add feet and yards, but he can convert feet to yards or yards to feet and then add like units.

Measurement is important in most occupations. A plumber measures the diameter of a length of pipe. A cabinetmaker measures the width of a piece of wood. A tailor measures a hem length.

The same like-unit rule can be applied to algebra. In algebra, you can add like terms, but you cannot add unlike terms. In this chapter, you will study this rule and many other important rules of algebra.

Some Unusual Units of Measures

Used in Shipping
5 cubic feet = 1 barrel bulk

Used in Printing
25 sheets of paper = 1 quire

Used for Surveying Land
7.92 inches = 1 link

Used for Measuring Depth of Water
6 feet = 1 fathom

Used for Weighing Jewelry
1 ounce = 20 pennyweight

↴2•1 Recognizing Like Terms and Unlike Terms

IN THIS LESSON, YOU WILL LEARN

To recognize the difference between like terms and unlike terms

WORDS TO LEARN

Terms *the parts of a variable expression separated by addition or subtraction signs*

Coefficient *the numerical part of a term that is not an exponent*

Like terms *terms whose variable parts are the same*

Unlike terms *terms whose variable parts are not the same*

The key on the left opens a padlock.
Which key on the right opens the same padlock? Why?

New Idea

The middle key at the right opens the padlock. It matches the key in the picture on the left. You could tell the two keys are alike by comparing their shapes. You can compare the parts of variable expressions just as you compared the parts of the keys. In algebra, we work with variable expressions. **Terms** (termz) are the parts of a variable expression that are separated by addition or subtraction signs. The numerical part of a term is called the **coefficient** (koh-uh-FIHSH-uhnt). If a term has no numerical part, then the coefficient is the number 1.

Example: How many terms are in this variable expression? What is the coefficient of each? $3x + 4x^2 + x^2y^2$

The expression has three terms, $3x$, $4x^2$, and x^2y^2. The coefficient of the first term is 3. The coefficient of the second term is 4. The coefficient of the third term is 1.

Terms with the same variable parts are called **like terms** (lyek termz). Terms with different variable parts are called **unlike terms** (un-LYEK termz).

These are like terms		These are unlike terms	
$17x$ and x	$6a$ and $25a$	$17x$ and $2x^2$	$3a^2$ and $9a$

Focus on the Idea

In variable expressions, like terms have the same variable parts. Unlike terms have different variable parts.

Practice

Rewrite each expression without a raised dot. The first one is done for you.

1. $6 \cdot y$ ___6y___

2. $3 \cdot n$ _____

3. $15 \cdot h \cdot p$ _____

4. $w \cdot d$ _____

Tell how many terms are in each expression.

5. $x + 5y$ _____

6. $k - 4$ _____

7. $ab^2 + ab + a$ _____

8. $m - n + 2m$ _____

Name the terms in each expression.

9. $5x + 6y$ _____

10. $k + 3d^4$ _____

Write *like* or *unlike* to describe the terms in each expression.

11. $14x + 4y$ _____

12. $2.5m + 65n$ _____

13. $20p^5 + b$ _____

14. $\frac{1}{2}c + 3\frac{3}{4}d$ _____

Are the terms alike? Write *yes* or *no*.

15. $4x, 5x$ _____

16. $18p, 6\frac{1}{2}p$ _____

17. $2mn, 2mn^2$ _____

18. $7k, k$ _____

Apply the Idea

19. Cheryl wrote this expression for the total number of grams of fat in a hamburger, french fries, and a milk shake: $30h + 18f + 9m$. Name the coefficients in Cheryl's expression.

_____

Write About It

20. Explain how like terms and unlike terms differ from each other.

_____

_____

_____

2•2 Understanding the Properties of Numbers

IN THIS LESSON, YOU WILL LEARN
To identify and use number properties

WORDS TO LEARN

Property *a rule involving an operation on numbers*

Commutative Property *states that the order in which numbers are added or multiplied does not change the sum or product*

Associative Property *states that the way in which numbers are grouped does not change the sum or product*

Identity Property *describes the results of adding 0 to a number or multiplying a number by 1*

Multiplicative Property of Zero *states that any number multiplied by 0 has a product of 0*

Imagine a parking lot with cars parked in 3 rows, 7 cars in each row. Or, imagine the cars parked in 7 rows, with 3 cars in each.

$3 \cdot 7 = 21$ cars $7 \cdot 3 = 21$ cars

Why are the two products equal?

New Idea

A **property** (PRAHP-uhr-tee) is a rule about an operation on numbers. The following properties describe some things about numbers. Look for patterns.

Commutative Property of Addition (kuh-MYOOT-uh-tihv PRAHP-uhr-tee)
The order in which numbers are added does not change the sum.

$$3 + 8 = 8 + 3$$

Commutative Property of Multiplication
The order in which numbers are multiplied does not change the product.

$$5 \cdot 2 = 2 \cdot 5$$

Associative Property of Addition (uh-SOH-shee-ayt-ihv PRAHP-uhr-tee)
The way in which numbers are grouped does not change the sum.

$$(2 + 6) + 3 = 2 + (6 + 3)$$

Associative Property of Multiplication
The way in which numbers are grouped does not change the product.

$$(4 \cdot 2) \cdot 7 = 4 \cdot (2 \cdot 7)$$

Identity Property of Addition (eye-DEHN-tuh-tee PRAHP-uhr-tee)
Adding 0 to a number does not change the number.
$$3 + 0 = 3$$

Identity Property of Multiplication
Multiplying a number by 1 does not change the number.
$$9 \cdot 1 = 9$$

Multiplicative Property of Zero (MUL-tuh-plih-kayt-ihv PRAHP-uhr-tee)
Multiplying a number by 0 gives a product of zero.
$$0 \cdot 5 = 0$$

The Commutative Property of Multiplication explains why, in the parking lot problem, $3 \cdot 7 = 7 \cdot 3$.

Focus on the Idea
Number properties for addition and multiplication describe patterns for finding sums and products.

Practice

Complete each statement. Use a number property to help.

1. $9 + 6 = 6 +$ _____

2. $7 \cdot$ _____ $= 7$

3. $(5 + 8) +$ _____ $= 5 + (8 + 9)$

4. _____ $\cdot 13 = 13 \cdot 15$

Name the property shown. The first one is done for you.

5. $16 \cdot 13 = 13 \cdot 16$ _____Commutative Property of Multiplication_____

6. $k + 0 = k$ _____

7. $(24 + m) + y = 24 + (m + y)$ _____

8. $t = t \cdot 1$ _____

9. $5.7 \cdot (3.2 \cdot c) = (5.7 \cdot 3.2) \cdot c$ _____

Apply the Idea

10. At a hardware store, Megan makes purchases of $4.25, $1.29, and $1.75. Which number properties could Megan use to find the sum mentally? Show how.

_____

Write About It

11. Choose one of the number properties discussed in this lesson. Explain what the property means and give examples of it.

_____

_____

2•3 Understanding the Distributive Property of Multiplication Over Addition

IN THIS LESSON, YOU WILL LEARN

To identify and use the Distributive Property of Multiplication over Addition

WORDS TO LEARN

Factor *a number multiplied by another number to produce a product*

Distributive Property of Multiplication Over Addition *states that a product can be found by adding, then multiplying, or by multiplying, then adding*

A garage measures 18 feet by 12 feet. A building contractor is adding a 6-foot extension at the rear of the building. Which method can she use to find the total area of the extended garage?

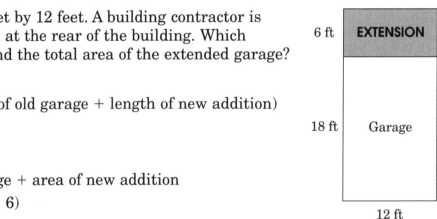

Method 1

Area = width • (length of old garage + length of new addition)

= 12(18 + 6)

Method 2

Area = area of old garage + area of new addition

= (12 • 18) + (12 • 6)

New Idea

Each number or variable you multiply is called a **factor** (FAK-tuhr).

Examples: Name the factors in each expression.

3 • 7   3 and 7 are factors.

3(a + b)   3 and (a + b) are factors.

The Distributive Property of Multiplication Over Addition (dih-STRIH-yoo-tihv PRAHP-uhr-tee) describes how a product can be found by either adding, then multiplying the factors, or by multiplying, then adding.

Example: Solve the garage problem using the Distributive Property of Multiplication Over Addition.

Method 1 $12(18 + 6) = 12 \cdot 24 = 288$

Method 2 $12 \cdot 18 + 12 \cdot 6 = 216 + 72 = 288$

The area of the extended garage is 288 square feet. Both methods give the same answer.

Focus on the Idea

The Distributive Property of Multiplication Over Addition states that each term inside the parentheses may be multiplied by the factor outside the parentheses. The products may then be added.

Practice

Name the factors in each expression. The first one is done for you.

1. $6 \cdot 9$ ___6 and 9___

2. $4(3)(2)$ _____

3. $8x$ _____

Complete each statement.

4. $7(9 + 5) =$ _____ $\cdot 9 +$ _____ $\cdot 5$

5. _____ $(2 + 6) = 3 \cdot 2 + 3 \cdot 6$

6. $5($_____ $+$ _____$) = 5d + 5am$

Rewrite each expression without parentheses.

7. $3(9 + 4)$ _____

8. $15(8 + 7)$ _____

9. $8(a + b)$ _____

10. $12.7(d + w)$ _____

Rewrite each expression using parentheses.

11. $4x + 4y$ _____

12. $13k + 13ab$ _____

Apply the Idea

13. Fourteen workers are on an assembly line. Each assembles 102 lamps in a day. The total number of lamps can be represented by $14(102)$. Think of 102 as $100 + 2$. Then find the product mentally.

_____

Write About It

14. Explain how to use a number property to express $6(a + b)$ as a sum.

_____

↴2•4 Adding Like Terms

Harvey has a 25-minute bus ride to his job each morning. He spends 8 hours at work. After work, he does his grocery shopping, so it takes him 40 minutes to get home. Which of the following expresses the total amount of time he is away from home?

  a. 25 min + 8 h + 40 min = 73 min

  b. 25 min + 8 h + 40 min = 9 h, 5 min

New Idea

You can add units that are alike, but you cannot add units that are unlike. Hours and minutes are unlike. To add them, you must first either change hours to minutes or minutes to hours.

$$25 \text{ min} + 8 \text{ h} + 40 \text{ min} = 8 \text{ h}, 65 \text{ min}$$

$$= 9 \text{ h}, 5 \text{ min}$$

Adding the terms of a variable expression is similar. You can add like terms, but you cannot add unlike terms. To add two or more like terms, add their coefficients.

To **simplify** (SIHM-pluh-fy) a variable expression means to combine its like terms, then to perform as many operations as possible. When like terms are added, the variables stay the same.

Examples: Simplify. $5y + 9y$ $7k^2 + 3k^2 + 6n$ $2a + 3a^2$

$5y + 9y = 14y$ ←like terms

$7k^2 + 3k^2 + 6n = 10k^2 + 6n$ ←like terms

$2a + 3a^2$ ←unlike terms

Since unlike terms cannot be added, $2a + 3a^2$ is already in simplest form.

↴Focus on the Idea

To add like terms, add their coefficients. Use the same variable. You cannot add unlike terms.

Practice

Can you add the terms? Write *yes* or *no*. The first two are done for you.

1. $3x + 5x$ ___yes___
2. $5a + 12a^2$ ___no___
3. $2k + 3k$ _____
4. $13pq + 15pq$ _____
5. $9m^2n + 4mn^2$ _____
6. $10y + y$ _____

Simplify by adding.

7. $3p + 6p$ _____
8. $12y + 14y$ _____
9. $8n + n$ _____
10. $15a + 18a + 6b$ _____
11. $c + 7c + 8c + 6 + 5$ _____
12. $4x + 3x + 2y + 5y$ _____
13. $5\frac{1}{2}k + 8\frac{1}{2}k + 3n + 12 + 25$ _____
14. $11.7a + 5.3a + 13.8b + 6.7b$ _____

Apply the Idea

15. Kuan installs smoke and carbon monoxide detectors in apartment buildings. He charges m dollars for each smoke detector and n dollars for each carbon monoxide detector. In one building, he installed 12 smoke detectors and 9 carbon monoxide detectors. In another building, he installed 15 smoke detectors and 7 carbon monoxide detectors.

    a. Write variable expressions for the amount Kuan charges for the detectors installed in each building.

    _____

    b. Add the expressions to find the total amount he charged for the detectors.

    _____

Write About It

16. Explain how to simplify the expression $5m + 7m + 9m^2$.

    _____

    _____

    _____

⬤2●5 Subtracting Like Terms

Ruth is an admitting clerk in the Metro Hospital emergency room. She has reduced the average time she needs to admit a patient from 16 minutes to 14 minutes. One day she admits n patients. How much time does she save by using her faster admitting method?

New Idea

You can subtract like terms by subtracting their coefficients and using the same **variable**. (See Lesson 1●1.) You cannot subtract unlike terms.

⟡Remember

Like terms have the same variable parts. Unlike terms have different variable parts.

Examples: Simplify. $15k - 4k$

Since $15k$ and $4k$ are like terms, subtract their coefficients.

$15k - 4k = 11k$

Simplify. $7p^2 + 6p + 2h - 3p^2$

Since $7p^2$ and $3p^2$ are the only like terms, subtract their coefficients. Leave the other terms the same.

$$7p^2 + 6p + 2h - 3p^2 = (7p^2 - 3p^2) + 6p + 2h$$
$$= 4p^2 + 6p + 2h$$

Using the old method of admitting patients, Ruth needed $16n$ minutes to admit n patients. Using the faster method, she needs $14n$ minutes to admit n patients. Time saved: $16n - 14n = 2n$ min.

◀Focus on the Idea

To subtract like terms, subtract their coefficients. Keep the same variable. You cannot subtract unlike terms.

Practice

Can you subtract the terms? Write *yes* or *no*. The first one is done for you.

1. $8x - 5y$ _____no_____
2. $13a^3 - 10a^3$ _____
3. $10n - 4n$ _____
4. $3ab - 2a$ _____
5. $7m^2n - 7m^2n$ _____
6. $23e - e$ _____

Simplify by subtracting.

7. $9g - 5g$ _____
8. $12u - 11u$ _____
9. $18w - 3w$ _____
10. $4x - 4x$ _____
11. $8.5a - 3.6a$ _____
12. $5\frac{1}{2}t - 4\frac{1}{3}t$ _____
13. $11k - 3k - 4k$ _____
14. $25a - 14a - 5a^2$ _____

Simplify.

15. $36h^2 + 14h - 19h^2 + 11h + 5 + 4$

_____

16. $2.4ab - 1.8ab + 3.5a^2b + 1.7ab^2 + 2.9a^2b$

_____

17. $4\frac{1}{4}x^2 + 5\frac{2}{3}x - 5\frac{2}{3}x + 2\frac{3}{4}x^2$

_____

Apply the Idea

18. From 1990 to 1994, the daily basic cost of a private room at Metro Hospital rose from \$600 to \$680. There are r private rooms in the hospital. Write a variable expression for how much more money the hospital received daily for all the rooms in 1994 than it did in 1990.

_____

Write About It

19. Subtraction is the inverse operation of addition. Explain how you can use this fact to check this subtraction: $9a - 4a = 5a$.

_____

_____

_____

⬇2•6 Multiplying Terms

⬆IN THIS LESSON, YOU WILL LEARN
To simplify algebraic expressions by multiplying like terms

WORDS TO LEARN
Monomial *a term that is a number, a variable, or the product of a number and one or more variables*

People use formulas for many activities. Many useful formulas involve simple operations. Three of these are:

distance = rate • time or $D = rt$
earnings = rate per hour • hours worked, or $E = rh$
area = length • width or $A = lw$

To use formulas, you must know how to replace variables with numbers. You must also know how to simplify expressions that contain both variables and numbers.

New Idea

A **monomial** (moh-NOH-mee-uhl) is a term that is a number, a variable, or the product of a number and one or more variables.

These are monomials.	These are not monomials.
6, a, $9m$, $5k^2$, $14xy$	$7 + n$, $\frac{x}{2}$, $9a - 3a$

To multiply any two monomials, first multiply their coefficients. Then multiply their variables.

Examples: Simplify. Use the properties of multiplication.

$$(7)(3n) = (7)(3)(n)$$
$$= 21n$$

$$(2c)(3d) = (2)(c)(3)(d)$$
$$= (2)(3)(c)(d)$$
$$= 6cd$$

$$(8ab)(5b) = (8)(a)(b)(5)(b)$$
$$= (8)(5)(a)(b)(b)$$
$$= 40ab^2$$

$$(xy)(xy) = (x)(y)(x)(y)$$
$$= (x)(x)(y)(y)$$
$$= x^2y^2$$

⬅Remember
$(b)(b) = b^2$ is read as "b squared."

⬆Focus on the Idea
To multiply two monomials, first multiply the coefficients, then multiply the variables.

Practice

Is the term a monomial? Write *yes* or *no*. The first one is done for you.

1. $6x$ ___*yes*___

2. 19 _____

3. $a + e$ _____

4. $3mn$ _____

5. $7y - 4$ _____

6. $25x^2y$ _____

Simplify by multiplying.

7. $(4a)(7b)$ _____

8. $(3x)(5y)$ _____

9. $(9m)(4n)$ _____

10. $(8p)(7p)$ _____

11. $(10k)(2k)$ _____

12. $(2h)(14k)$ _____

13. $(c)(3c)$ _____

14. $(ab)(ab)$ _____

15. $(7st)(3t)$ _____

16. $(12)(3mn)$ _____

17. $(2h)(15)$ _____

18. $(8x)(3xyz)$ _____

Find the following for the terms $9c$ and $5c$.

19. the sum _____

20. the difference _____

21. the product _____

Apply the Idea

22. A package of mailing envelopes contains m envelopes. At its January Clearance Sale, one of the Office City stores sold $36m$ envelopes for x dollars per package. If each of the 120 Office City stores sells 36 packages, write an expression for the total cost of those envelopes.

_____

Write About It

23. Explain how you would find the product of $5h$ and $7w$.

_____

_____

_____

_____

►2•7 Dividing Terms

►IN THIS LESSON, YOU WILL LEARN

To simplify algebraic expressions by dividing like terms

WORDS TO LEARN

Inverse operation *an operation that reverses the result of another operation*

Julio is a computer consultant. He earns \$75 per hour. How many hours did Julio work if he earned \$56,250?

New Idea

You know how to multiply two monomials. You also know that division is the **inverse operation** of multiplication. (See Lesson 1•5.) This means that you can divide two monomials by reversing the process of multiplication.

Multiply: $3x \cdot 4y = 12xy$
Divide: $12xy \div 4y = 3x$

You can divide two monomials by first dividing their coefficients, then dividing their variables. This is usually easier to see if you rewrite the division example as a fraction.

Examples: Divide. $12xy \div 4y$

Rewrite $12xy \div 4y$ as $\frac{12xy}{4y} = \frac{12}{4} \cdot \frac{x}{1} \cdot \frac{y}{y}$

$$= 3 \cdot x \cdot 1$$

$$= 3x$$

Divide to find out how many hours (h) Julio worked.

$\$75h = \$56,250$

$\frac{75h}{75} = \frac{56,250}{75}$ ←Divide both sides by 75.

$h = 750$

Julio worked 750 hours.

►Focus on the Idea

To divide two monomials, first divide the coefficients, then divide the variables.

Practice

Rewrite as a fraction. The first one is done for you.

1. $24 \div 6$ — $\frac{24}{6}$ or $\frac{4}{1}$

2. $18 \div 2$ _____

3. $x \div y$ _____

4. $3x \div 5$ _____

5. $12n^2 \div 2n$ _____

6. $abc \div ab$ _____

Simplify by dividing.

7. $36h \div 6$ _____

8. $20m \div m$ _____

9. $\frac{24k}{2}$ _____

10. $\frac{9a}{3a}$ _____

11. $\frac{cd}{d}$ _____

12. $\frac{15p}{15p}$ _____

13. $\frac{6a^2}{3a}$ _____

14. $\frac{27x^2}{9x^2}$ _____

15. $\frac{50m^2n^2}{10mn^2}$ _____

16. $\frac{7ab^2c}{7a}$ _____

17. By what monomial would you multiply $3ab^2c$ to get the product $18ab^2c^2$? _____

Apply the Idea

18. Ali is a bookkeeper. He has to make sure there is enough money in the payroll account to pay the employees. He needs $2,000 for each of the n employees per week.

    a. If there is $64,000 in the account, how many employees can Ali pay in one week? _____

    b. If there is $128,000$mn^2$ in the account and the number of employees is $16mn$, how many weeks' pay is in the account? _____

Write About It

19. Explain how you can use multiplication to check the answer to a division problem.

    _____

    _____

    _____

    _____

Chapter 2   Review

In This Chapter, You Have Learned

- To recognize the difference between like terms and unlike terms
- To identify and use number properties
- To simplify algebraic expressions by adding, subtracting, multiplying, and dividing like terms

Words You Know

From the lists of "Words to Learn," choose the word or phrase that best completes each statement.

1. The equation $3(x + y) = 3x + 3y$ illustrates the _____ Property _____.
2. In the term $5a^2$, the number 5 is the _____.
3. In the product $2 \cdot 7$, both 2 and 7 are _____.

More Practice

Name the terms and the coefficients in each expression.

4. $2x + 3y - 5z$ terms _____

                                coefficients _____

5. $4m^3 + 7m^2 - 9.2m + 16$ terms _____

                                coefficients _____

Write _like_ or _unlike_ to describe each pair of terms.

6. $8k, \quad 26x$ _____   7. $3h, \quad 9\frac{1}{2}h$ _____

8. $5ab, \quad 6ab$ _____   9. $18m^2n, \quad 18m^2np$ _____

Simplify.

10. $11k + 9k$ _____   11. $2.4x + 6.6x$ _____

12. $n + n$ _____   13. $23h - 14h$ _____

14. $30e + 20e - 15e$ _____   15. $3a + 4a + 5b$ _____

16. $14n - 6n + 3m$ _____   17. $7p - (5p - 4p)$ _____

18. $2y(5y)$ _____   19. $3p \cdot 2p$ _____

20. $8a \cdot 5c$ _____   21. $dv(3dv)$ _____

22. $5m(6mn)$ _____   23. $10ab \div 2a$ _____

24. $24\frac{xyz}{3y}$ _____   25. $\frac{13t}{13t}$ _____

26. $4ab + 5ab + a + 3a + 6 + 7$ _____

27. $3x^2y + 7x^2y + 11x - 3x + 10y - 9y$ _____

28. Find the sum, difference, product, and quotient of the monomials $12n$ and $4n$.

_____

Name the property shown.

29. $7 + 0 = 7$ _____

30. $mn = nm$ _____

31. $(4 + 7) + 11 = 4 + (7 + 11)$ _____

32. $(h + k) + 7 = (k + h) + 7$ _____

Use the Distributive Property of Multiplication Over Addition to write each expression without parentheses.

33. $6(x + y)$ _____   **34.** $2a(3a + 4b + 5c)$ _____

Problems You Can Solve

35. A flashlight costs d dollars. One customer bought 3 flashlights. Another customer bought 5 flashlights.

   a. Write expressions for the cost of the flashlights bought by each customer. _____

   b. Write an expression for the total cost to both customers.

   _____

36. **For Your Portfolio**   For one day, keep track of your activities that involve adding or subtracting like terms. Record ten of your own activities in a chart like this one. For each activity, write a question, identify the like terms, decide whether to add or subtract, then give the sum or difference

Activity	Question	Like Terms	Sum? Difference?
1. Spent 25 minutes traveling to school and 18 minutes traveling home.	How much time did I spend traveling?	25 minutes 18 minutes	sum; 43 minutes
2. Spent $1.50 on today's lunch and $3.75 on yesterday's lunch.	How much time did I spend on lunch yesterday?	3.75 dollars, 1.50 dollars	difference; 2.25 dollars

Chapter 2   Practice Test

Use this expression. $3x^2 + 2x - 5pr$

1. Name the terms in the expression. _____

2. Name the coefficients in the expression. _____

Simplify.

3. $5t + 3t$ _____   4. $21x - 13x$ _____

5. $x + x + 3x$ _____   6. $14de + 3de$ _____

7. $18n - (10n + 2n)$ _____   8. $y - y$ _____

9. $5a - 6b + 7a + 8b + 11$ _____

10. $8x^2 + y^2 + 15xy + 13x^2 + 11xy + 3y^2$ _____

Simplify each expression by multiplying or dividing monomials.

11. $3(7a)$ _____   12. $4x(3y)$ _____

13. $2k \cdot 3k$ _____   14. $(2x)(5xy)$ _____

15. $18a \div 3$ _____   16. $\frac{32h}{h}$ _____

17. $\frac{9xy}{9y}$ _____   18. $\frac{44abc^2}{4ac}$ _____

19. Find the sum, difference, product, and quotient of the monomials $15y$ and $3y$.

_____

_____

Name the property shown.

20. $a \cdot (b \cdot c) = (a \cdot b) \cdot c$ _____

21. $k(1) = k$ _____

22. $m + 3e = 3e + m$ _____

Use the Distributive Property of Multiplication Over Addition to write each expression without parentheses.

23. $4(a + b)$ _____   24. $2x(x + 3y)$ _____

25. A rectangular rug measures $3d$ yards by $2d$ yards.
    a. What is the area of the rug? _____
    b. The rug sells for $25 per square yard. What is the cost of the rug? _____

Chapter 3
Equations and Formulas

◢ OBJECTIVES:

In this chapter, you will learn

- *To recognize an equation and its solution*
- *To solve equations mentally*
- *To solve and check equations of the form*
  $x + a = b, x - a = b, ax = b,$ and $\frac{x}{a} = b$
- *To recognize that a formula is a type of equation*
- *To solve equations containing fractions and mixed numbers*

From the time that we are very young, balance is important to us. One sure sign of this is the many ways we use the word *balance* when we speak.

"To be a star running back in football, you've got to have great *balance*."

"My car shimmies when it reaches 40 miles per hour. I think I need to *balance* my tires."

One of the rules of balance is shown by a two-pan balance. When one side has more weight on it than the other, the device is out of balance. To be brought back into balance, weight must be either added to the lighter side or taken away from the heavier side. To stay in balance, anything done to one side must be done to the other side, too.

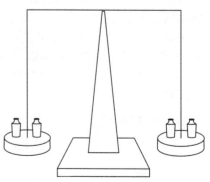

In this chapter, you will solve equations in much the same way as a mechanic keeps cars from shimmying—by using the rules of balance.

3•1 What Is an Equation?

IN THIS LESSON, YOU WILL LEARN

To recognize an equation and its solution

To solve equations mentally

WORDS TO LEARN

Algebraic sentence *a statement that contains numbers or variables*

Equation *a sentence that contains an equal sign*

Open sentence *an equation that contains a variable*

Solution *the value of a variable that makes an open sentence true*

Akira works as a stockroom clerk for an electronics supply company. When he works overtime, he receives 1.5 times his regular hourly wage. His overtime wage is $9 per hour. Write an equation you could solve to find his regular hourly wage.

New Idea

Any statement that contains numbers or variables is an **algebraic sentence** (al-juh-BRAY-ihk SEHN-tuhns). If a sentence has an equal sign, it is an **equation** (ee-KWAY-zhuhn). An equation can be true or false.

true equation: $3 + 4 = 7$ false equation: $11 - 6 = 4$

An equation that has a variable is an **open sentence** (OH-puhn SEHN-tuhns). An open sentence can be true or false, depending on the value of the variable.

$$x + 5 = 8 \qquad \leftarrow \text{open sentence}$$
$$3 + 5 = 8 \qquad \leftarrow \text{If } x = 3, \text{ the sentence is true.}$$
$$4 + 5 = 8 \qquad \leftarrow \text{If } x = 4, \text{ the sentence is false.}$$

Any value of a variable that makes an open sentence true is a **solution** (suh-LOO-shuhn) to the equation. You can check if your solution is correct by substituting it for the variable in an open sentence, then computing. If your solution is correct, you will get a true sentence. Some open sentences or equations can be solved mentally.

Examples: Solve for the variable. $x + 9 = 30$ $3d = 21$

$x + 9 = 30$ Think: What number added to 9 equals 30? The answer is 21.

$3d = 21$ Think: What number multiplied by 3 equals 21? The answer is 7.

1. Miranda says 5 is the solution to $4x = 20$. Is she right? Explain.

_____

_____

◣ **Focus on the Idea**

An open sentence contains a variable. A solution is the value for the variable that makes an open sentence true.

Practice

Write *true*, *false*, or *open* for each sentence. The first one is done for you.

2. $6(8) = 56$ ___false___

3. $3 + k = 15$ _____

4. $5 + 2 \cdot 3 = 21$ _____

5. $36 \div 9 \div 2 = 2$ _____

Of the values listed, underline the one that is a solution to the equation.

6. $x - 9 = 2$; 11, 7, 18

7. $3n = 12$; 15, 9, 4

8. $\frac{m}{3} = 6$; 18, 2, 3

9. $2x + 1 = 7$; 12, 3, 2

Solve each equation mentally.

10. $v + 5 = 9$ $v =$ _____

11. $20 - k = 9$ $k =$ _____

12. $6p = 42$ $p =$ _____

13. $11 = b + 11$ $b =$ _____

14. $\frac{a}{3} = 12$ $a =$ _____

15. $2h = 7$ $h =$ _____

16. $6(y + 1) = 18$ $y =$ _____

17. $\frac{4x}{2} = 8$ $x =$ _____

Apply the Idea

18. Reread the problem at the beginning of the lesson.

    a. Let $w =$ Akira's regular hourly wage. Write an open sentence you can solve to find w. _____

    b. Solve the equation mentally. What is Akira's regular hourly wage? _____

✏ Write About It

19. Explain how you can decide if a number is a solution to an open sentence.

_____

_____

◀3•2 Subtracting to Solve Equations

Dawn got a consumer loan from her bank to buy a computer. The price of the computer is $1,650. With the interest and **finance costs** (FY-nans kawsts), Dawn must repay $1,835 to the bank. Find the amount of the interest and finance costs of Dawn's loan.

New Idea

Many equations are too difficult to solve mentally. You can use inverse operations to solve such equations. You must keep an equation balanced by using the inverse operation on both sides of the equation.

Example: Write and solve an equation to help find the amount that the bank is charging Dawn for the loan. Check your work.

Let c = the amount of the charges.
Then $c + \$1,650 = \$1,835$.

Use an inverse operation to solve the equation. Subtraction is the inverse operation for addition.

$$c + 1,650 = 1,835 \qquad \leftarrow \text{Equation}$$

$$c + 1,650 - 1,650 = 1,835 - 1,650 \leftarrow \text{Subtract 1,650 from both sides of the equation.}$$

$$c = 185$$

$$\text{Check:} \quad c + 1,650 = 1,835 \qquad \leftarrow \text{Substitute 185 for } c.$$

$$185 + 1,650 \stackrel{?}{=} 1,835$$

$$1,835 = 1,835 \qquad \leftarrow \text{The solution checks.}$$

The bank is charging Dawn $185 for the loan.

Focus on the Idea

To solve an equation of the form x + a = b, subtract the value of a from both sides of the equation.

Practice

Tell how you can use subtraction to solve each equation. Do not solve. The first one is done for you.

1. $x + 5 = 7$ _____Subtract 5 from both sides._____

2. $v + 14 = 20$ _____

3. $8 + y = 31$ _____

4. $9 = x + 2$ _____

5. $20.4 = 13.7 + k$ _____

Use subtraction to solve the equation. Check your answer. The first one is done for you.

6. $h + 6 = 15$
$h + 6 - 6 = 15 - 6$
$h = 9$

   Check: $h + 6 = 15$
   $9 + 6 \stackrel{?}{=} 15$
   $15 = 15$

7. $d + 2 = 5$

   Check:

8. $s + 9 = 14$

   Check:

9. $n + 4.5 = 8$

   Check:

10. $86 = g + 39$

    Check:

11. $777 = 345 + k$

    Check:

Apply the Idea

12. A $35 sweater is on sale for $29.95. Let r stand for regular price and s stand for sale price.

    a. Use the formula to write an equation you can solve to find the discount (d). _____

    b. Find the discount. _____

Write About It

13. Explain how you might use a balance, counters, and an envelope to demonstrate solving the equation $x + 4 = 9$.

    _____

    _____

▼3•3 Adding to Solve Equations

IN THIS LESSON, YOU WILL LEARN

To solve and check equations of the form x − a = b

WORDS TO LEARN

Blueprint *a diagram showing the shape and measurements of an object*

To pay his electric bill, James writes a check for $34.91. After subtracting, his new balance is $435.29. What was his old balance?

New Idea

In the last lesson, you solved addition equations by subtracting. In this lesson, because addition and subtraction are inverse operations, you can solve subtraction equations by adding.

Example: Write an equation to find James's old balance.

Let b = the old balance in James's checking account. Then $b - \$34.91 = \$435.29$.

You can now use an inverse operation to solve the equation by adding the same amount to both sides.

$$b - 34.91 = 435.29 \qquad \leftarrow\text{Equation}$$

$$b - 34.91 + 34.91 = 435.29 + 34.91 \leftarrow \text{Add 34.91 to both sides of the equation.}$$

$$b = 470.20$$

Check: $b - 34.91 = 435.29$

$$470.20 - 34.91 \stackrel{?}{=} 435.29 \qquad \leftarrow \text{Substitute 470.20 for } b.$$

$$435.29 = 435.29 \qquad \leftarrow \text{The solution checks.}$$

James's old checking account balance was $470.20.

Focus on the Idea

To solve an equation of the form $x - a = b$, add the value of a to both sides of the equation.

Practice

Tell how you can use addition to solve each equation. Do not solve. The first one is done for you.

1. $p - 3 = 4$ _____Add 3 to both sides._____

2. $a - 7.5 = 19$ _____

3. $15 = y - 5$ _____

Use addition to solve each equation. Check your answer. The first one is done for you.

4.
$$h - 3 = 5$$
$$h - 3 + 3 = 5 + 3$$
$$h = 8$$

Check: $h - 3 = 5$
$$8 - 3 \stackrel{?}{=} 5$$
$$5 = 5$$

5. $s - 6 = 12$

Check:

6. $c - 8 = 12$

Check:

7. $y - 3.7 = 4.6$

Check:

8. $11 = e - 12$

Check:

9. $131 = x - 257$

Check:

Apply the Idea

10. A **blueprint** (BLOO-prihnt), a diagram used to make machine parts, shows that the length of a part should measure 3.26 centimeters. The finished part may measure up to 0.13 centimeters longer than 3.26 and still be acceptable.

    a. Let l equal the greatest acceptable finished length of the manufactured part. To find l write an equation that you can solve using addition. _____

    b. Solve the equation. _____

Write About It

11. Write a problem you could solve using $x - 3 = 10$.

_____

_____

3•4 Dividing to Solve Equations

IN THIS LESSON, YOU WILL LEARN
To solve and check equations of the form ax = b

WORDS TO LEARN
Multiplicative inverse *a number times its multiplicative inverse equals 1*

Inverting *interchanging the numerator and the denominator of a fraction*

A carpenter purchases twenty-five 12-foot-long two-by-fours. The charge is $85. What is the price of one of the two-by-fours?

New Idea

Addition and subtraction equations can be solved by using inverse operations. Inverse operations can also be used to solve equations in which a variable is *multiplied* by a number. Such equations can be solved by using *division*, the inverse operation for multiplication.

Example: Write an equation to find the cost of one two-by-four.

Let p = the price of one two-by-four.
Then, write the equation $25p = 85$.

$$25p = 85 \quad \leftarrow\text{Equation}$$

$$\frac{25p}{25} = \frac{85}{25} \quad \leftarrow\text{Divide both sides of the equation by 25.}$$

$$p = 3.4$$

Check: $25p = 85$

$$25(3.4) \stackrel{?}{=} 85 \quad \leftarrow\text{Substitute 3.4 for } p.$$

$$85 = 85 \quad \leftarrow\text{The solution checks.}$$

The price of one two-by-four is $3.40.

✓Check the Math

1. Dominick solved the equation $8y = 16$ and said that $y = 2$. How do you think Dominick found his answer? Is he correct?

When you use an inverse operation to solve an equation, always perform that same operation on both sides of the equation.

◤ Focus on the Idea

To solve an equation of the form ax = b, divide both sides of the equation by the value of a.

Practice

Tell how you can use division to solve each equation. Do not solve. The first one is done for you.

2. $4c = 24$ _____ Divide both sides by 4 _____

3. $7k = 35$ _____

4. $2.5p = 40$ _____

5. $75 = 12y$ _____

6. $36 = 4d$ _____

Use division to solve each equation. Check your answer. The first one is done for you.

7. $3a = 12$
$$\frac{3a}{3} = \frac{12}{3}$$
$$a = 4$$

8. $5n = 45$

9. $10m = 60$

Check: $3a = 12$
$3 \cdot 4 \overset{?}{=} 12$
$12 = 12$ √

Check:

Check:

10. $36 = 4d$

11. $12p = 144$

12. $91 = 7b$

Check:

Check:

Check:

13. $6k = 9$

14. $1.4x = 42$

15. $6.84 = 1.9s$

Check:

Check:

Check:

Extend the Idea

You have learned that you can use division to solve an equation in which a variable is multiplied by a number. Another method of solving this type of equation uses the **multiplicative inverse** (MUL-tuh-plih-kayt-ihv IHN-vers). When a number is multiplied by its multiplicative inverse, the product is 1.

Examples: Find the multiplicative inverse of 5.

The multiplicative inverse of 5 is $\frac{1}{5}$ because
$5 \cdot \frac{1}{5} = \frac{5}{5} = 1$.

You can find the multiplicative inverse of a fraction by interchanging the numerator and the denominator. Interchanging the numerator and the denominator is called **inverting** (ihn-VER-ting) the fraction.

Find the multiplicative inverse of $\frac{2}{3}$.

The multiplicative inverse of $\frac{2}{3}$ is $\frac{3}{2}$ because
$\frac{2}{3} \cdot \frac{3}{2} = \frac{6}{6} = 1$.

⤳Remember

To multiply fractions, just multiply the numerators and multiply the denominators.

Example: Solve. $\frac{3}{5}x = 12$

$$\frac{3}{5}x = 12 \qquad \leftarrow \text{Equation}$$

$$\frac{5}{3} \cdot \frac{3}{5}x = \frac{5}{3} \cdot \frac{12}{1} \leftarrow \text{Multiply both sides of the equation by } \frac{5}{3}, \text{ the multiplicative inverse of } \frac{3}{5}.$$

$$1x = \frac{5}{3} \cdot \frac{12}{1} \leftarrow \text{Product of } \frac{5}{3} \cdot \frac{3}{5} \text{ is 1.}$$

$$x = \frac{60}{3} \qquad \leftarrow \text{Simplify.}$$

$$x = 20$$

Check: $\frac{3}{5}x = 12$

$$\frac{3}{5} \cdot \frac{20}{1} \overset{?}{=} 12$$

$$\frac{60}{5} \overset{?}{=} 12$$

$$12 = 12 \qquad \leftarrow \text{The solution checks.}$$

Multiplying by the multiplicative inverse of a number is the same as dividing by the original number.

✓Check Your Understanding

16. Find the multiplicative inverse of 21. _____

Practice

Give the multiplicative inverse of each number. The first one is done for you.

17. $\frac{3}{4}$ $\frac{4}{3}$

18. $\frac{5}{6}$ _____

19. $\frac{1}{2}$ _____

20. $\frac{1}{9}$ _____

21. 15 _____

22. $\frac{8}{3}$ _____

Solve each equation using a multiplicative inverse. Check your answer. The first one is done for you.

23.

$$\frac{2}{3}x = 24$$
$$\left(\frac{3}{2}\right)\left(\frac{2}{3}\right)x = \left(\frac{24}{1}\right)\left(\frac{3}{2}\right)$$
$$1x = \frac{72}{2}$$
$$x = 36$$

Check: $\frac{2}{3}x = 24$
$$\left(\frac{2}{3}\right)(36) \stackrel{?}{=} 24$$
$$\left(\frac{2}{3}\right)\left(\frac{36}{1}\right) \stackrel{?}{=} 24$$
$$\frac{72}{3} \stackrel{?}{=} 24$$
$$24 = 24$$

24. $\frac{1}{6}y = 9$

Check:

25. $6.9 = \frac{3}{8}p$

26. $221 = \frac{13}{4}k$

Check:

Check:

Apply the Idea

27. A city bus driver's route is 7.6 miles long. It takes the driver $\frac{2}{3}$ hour to complete the route.

   a. Write an equation you could solve to find the driver's average speed. _____

   b. Solve the equation. _____

Write About It

28. Explain how dividing by 2 is the same as multiplying by $\frac{1}{2}$.

_____

_____

_____

3•5 Multiplying to Solve Equations

IN THIS LESSON, YOU WILL LEARN

To solve and check equations of the form $\frac{x}{a} = b$

WORDS TO LEARN

Ratio *a comparison of two numbers by division*
Proportion *an expression that states that two ratios are equal*

A mechanic works on Antonio's car. When Antonio receives the bill, he divides the total labor cost by the 3 hours the mechanic worked to get the mechanic's hourly rate. If the mechanic works at a rate of $48 per hour, what is the total labor charge?

New Idea

Since division is the inverse operation for multiplication, to solve an equation in which the variable is *divided* by a number, *multiply* both sides of the equation by that number.

Example: Write an equation to find the total charge for the mechanic's labor.

Let t = the total cost for labor.
Then write the equation $\frac{t}{3} = 48$.

$$\frac{t}{3} = 48 \qquad \leftarrow\text{Equation}$$

$$3\frac{t}{3} = (3)(48) \qquad \leftarrow\text{Multiply both sides of the equation by 3.}$$

$$t = 144$$

Check: $\frac{t}{3} = 48$

$$\frac{144}{3} \stackrel{?}{=} 48 \qquad \leftarrow\text{Substitute 144 for } t.$$

$$48 = 48 \qquad \leftarrow\text{The solution checks.}$$

The total labor charge is $144.

46 Chapter 3 *Equations and Formulas*

Focus on the Idea

To solve an equation of the form $\frac{x}{a} = b$, multiply both sides of the equation by the value of a.

Practice

Tell how you can use multiplication to solve each equation. Do not solve. The first one is done for you.

1. $\frac{h}{3} = 6$ _____Multiply both sides by 3._____

2. $\frac{n}{7} = 4$ _____

3. $\frac{b}{3.1} = 18$ _____

4. $12 = \frac{a}{5}$ _____

5. $\frac{x}{2} = 13$ _____

Use multiplication to solve each equation. Check your answer. The first one is done for you.

6.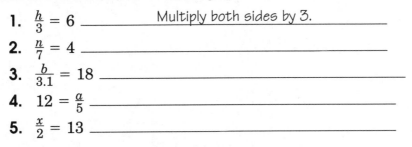
$$\frac{x}{2} = 6$$
$$2 \cdot \frac{x}{2} = 6 \cdot 2$$
$$x = 12$$

Check: $\frac{x}{2} = 6$

$\frac{12}{2} \overset{?}{=} 6$

$6 = 6$

7. $\frac{y}{9} = 5$

Check:

8. $\frac{p}{3} = 10$

Check:

9. $\frac{d}{12} = 7$

Check:

10. $11 = \frac{k}{3}$

Check:

11. $4.5 = \frac{a}{4}$

Check:

12. $\frac{e}{8.9} = 2.8$

Check:

13. $3 = \frac{n}{16}$

Check:

14. $33 = \frac{c}{17}$

Check:

15. $\dfrac{p}{17} = 8$ **16.** $\dfrac{v}{0.46} = 1.35$ **17.** $1 = \dfrac{w}{23.7}$

Check: Check: Check:

Extend the Idea

A **ratio** (RAY-shoh) is a comparison of two numbers by division. The ratio comparing 2 and 7 can be written three ways.

2 to 7   2 : 7 $\dfrac{2}{7}$

A **proportion** (proh-PAWR-shun) is a statement that two ratios are equal.

Here is one proportion that can be written for the ratio 2 to 7:

$$\dfrac{2}{7} = \dfrac{6}{21}$$

In a proportion, the cross-products are equal.

$$\dfrac{2}{7} \times \dfrac{6}{21}$$

$$2 \cdot 21 = 7 \cdot 6$$

$$42 = 42$$

Sometimes, one of the values in a proportion is missing. You can find the missing value by solving the proportion.

Example: Solve. $\dfrac{n}{45} = \dfrac{4}{9}$

$$\dfrac{n}{45} = \dfrac{4}{9} \qquad \leftarrow \text{Equation}$$

$$\dfrac{n}{45} \times \dfrac{4}{9} \qquad \leftarrow \text{Cross multiply.}$$

$$9n = 4 \cdot 45$$

$$9n = 180 \qquad \leftarrow \text{Divide both sides by 9.}$$

$$n = 20$$

Check: $\dfrac{n}{45} = \dfrac{4}{9}$

$$\dfrac{20}{45} \stackrel{?}{=} \dfrac{4}{9} \qquad \leftarrow \text{Substitute 20 for } n.$$

$$20 \cdot 9 \stackrel{?}{=} 45 \cdot 4 \leftarrow \text{Cross multiply.}$$

$$180 = 180 \qquad \leftarrow \text{The solution checks. The missing value in the proportion is } n = 20.$$

18. You can think of a proportion as two equal fractions. Explain two ways to solve this proportion. $\frac{3}{4} = \frac{x}{12}$

_____

Practice

Use multiplication to solve each proportion. Check your answer. The first one is done for you.

19. $\frac{x}{27} = \frac{7}{9}$ **20.** $\frac{m}{25} = \frac{9}{15}$ **21.** $\frac{32}{28} = \frac{y}{35}$

$9 \cdot x = 27 \cdot 7$

$9x = 189$

$x = 21$

Check: $\frac{x}{27} = \frac{7}{9}$ Check: Check:

$\frac{21}{27} \stackrel{?}{=} \frac{7}{9}$

$189 = 189$

22. $\frac{h}{10} = \frac{28}{16}$ **23.** $\frac{e}{25} = \frac{30}{125}$ **24.** $\frac{5}{15} = \frac{c}{24}$

Check: Check: Check:

Apply the Idea

25. The formula $I = \frac{V}{R}$ is used to find the current in an electrical circuit where I = current, V = voltage, and R = resistance. In one circuit, $R = 25$ ohms and $I = 4$ amperes.

     a. Write an equation you can use to find V, the number of volts in the circuit. _____

     b. Solve the equation to find the number of volts.

     _____

✎ Write About It

26. Explain how you could use inverse operations twice to solve this equation. $\frac{x}{2} + 4 = 7$

_____

_____

3•6 What Is a Formula?

A bricklayer is building a wall of the size shown. Six bricks are needed to cover each square foot of surface. Each brick costs $.75. Find the cost of the total number of bricks needed for the wall.

24 ft

5 ft

New Idea

A **formula** (FAWR-myoo-luh) gives the relationship between two or more variables. The following are examples of formulas.

$A = lw$ (area of a rectangle equals the length times the width)

$d = rt$ (distance traveled equals rate of speed times the amount of time traveled)

$s = r - d$ (sale price equals regular price minus discount)

A formula is an equation. If you are given values for all but one of the variables in a formula, you can solve for the remaining variable just as you would solve any equation.

Example: A trucker drove 150 miles at an average speed of 50 miles per hour. How long did the trip take?

$$d = rt \qquad \leftarrow \text{Choose the right formula.}$$

$$150 = 50t \qquad \leftarrow \text{Substitute values into the equation.}$$

$$\frac{150}{50} = \frac{50t}{50} \qquad \leftarrow \text{Divide both sides by 50.}$$

$$3 = t$$

Check: $150 = 50t$

$150 \stackrel{?}{=} 50 \cdot 3 \quad \leftarrow$ Substitute 3 for t.

$150 = 150 \qquad \leftarrow$ The solution checks.

The trip took 3 hours.

Focus on the Idea

A formula is an equation. To use a formula, substitute values for all variables except for the unknown. Then solve the equation for the unknown variable.

Practice

Write an equation by substituting the given values of the variables into the formula. Do not solve the equation. The first equation is written for you.

Formula	Given Values	Equation
1. Area of rectangle: $A = lw$	$A = 20, w = 2$	$20 = \ell(2)$
2. Distance: $d = rt$	$d = 300, r = 50$	_____
3. Perimeter of rectangle: $P = 2l + 2w$	$P = 34, l = 12$	_____
4. Sale price: $s = r - d$	$r = 84, d = 16$	_____
5. Temperature conversion: $F = 1.8C + 32$	$F = 96$	_____
6. Area of triangle: $A = \frac{1}{2}bh$	$A = 36, b = 8$	_____

Substitute the values of the variables into the formula. Then solve the equation for the remaining variable. The first one is done for you.

7. $s = r - d; s = 26, d = 5$ ___$26 = r - 5, r = 31$___

8. $d = rt; d = 45, t = 5$ _____

9. $A = lw; l = 2.5, w = 1.8$ _____

10. $F = 1.8C + 32; C = 55$ _____

11. $A = \frac{1}{2}bh; A = 12, b = 8$ _____

Apply the Idea

12. Look back at the problem about the bricks on page 50.

    a. Use the formula for the area of a rectangle to find the area of the wall. _____

    b. Find the number of bricks needed to build the wall.

    _____

    c. Find the cost of the wall. _____

Write About It

13. Why is a formula also an equation? Explain your answer.

_____

_____

One month a nurse had 72 patients with type O-positive blood. That was three-sevenths of his patients. How many patients did he have?

New Idea

To solve an equation containing a fraction or a **mixed number**, which is made up of a whole number and a fraction, first notice whether addition, subtraction, multiplication, or division is involved. Sometimes, you have to add or subtract fractions with different denominators. Other times, you have to change a mixed number to an **improper fraction**, a fraction with a numerator greater than or equal to its denominator. To solve, apply the inverse operation.

⟲Remember

To solve an equation in which multiplication is involved, you can multiply by the multiplicative inverse. Fractions must have the same denominator before they can be added or subtracted.

Examples: *Addition*

$$x + 1\tfrac{2}{3} = 11$$

$$x + 1\tfrac{2}{3} - 1\tfrac{2}{3} = 11 - 1\tfrac{2}{3}$$

$$x = 9\tfrac{1}{3}$$

Subtraction $d - \tfrac{7}{9} = 2\tfrac{3}{4}$

$$d - \tfrac{7}{9} + \tfrac{7}{9} = 2\tfrac{3}{4} + \tfrac{7}{9}$$

$$d = 3\tfrac{19}{36}$$

Multiplication $\quad 2\tfrac{1}{5}k = 4\tfrac{1}{2}$

$$\tfrac{11}{5}k = \tfrac{9}{2}$$

$$(\tfrac{5}{11})(\tfrac{11}{5})k = (\tfrac{5}{11})(\tfrac{9}{2})$$

$$k = \tfrac{45}{22} = 2\tfrac{1}{22}$$

Division $\quad\quad \tfrac{h}{9} = 6$

$$(9)(\tfrac{h}{9}) = (9)(6)$$

$$h = 54$$

Focus on the Idea

To solve an equation containing fractions or mixed numbers, apply the inverse operation.

Practice

Name the operation you can use to solve each equation. Do not solve. The first one is done for you.

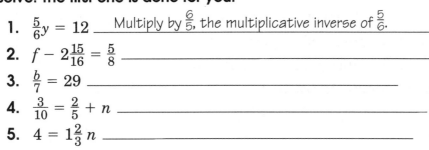

1. $\frac{5}{6}y = 12$ ___Multiply by $\frac{6}{5}$, the multiplicative inverse of $\frac{5}{6}$.___

2. $f - 2\frac{15}{16} = \frac{5}{8}$ _____

3. $\frac{b}{7} = 29$ _____

4. $\frac{3}{10} = \frac{2}{5} + n$ _____

5. $4 = 1\frac{2}{3}n$ _____

Solve each equation.

6. $x - \frac{7}{8} = 2\frac{1}{4}$

7. $\frac{4}{5}k = 54$

8. $18 = \frac{h}{7}$

9. $5\frac{5}{6} = 2\frac{1}{4} + y$

Apply the Idea

10. a. To make muffins, a baker uses $1\frac{7}{8}$ pounds more flour than he uses to make rolls. He uses $2\frac{1}{4}$ pounds to make rolls. Write and solve an equation to find how much flour he uses for muffins.

_____

b. The flour for the rolls costs $.81. Write and solve an equation to find the price of flour per pound.

_____

Write About It

11. Refer to page 52. Write and solve an equation to find the total number of the nurse's patients. Explain how you found the solution.

_____

_____

_____

Chapter 3 Review

In This Chapter, You Have Learned
- To recognize an equation and its solution
- To solve equations mentally
- To solve and check equations of the form $x + a = b$
- To solve and check equations of the form $x - a = b$
- To solve and check equations of the form $ax = b$
- To solve and check equations of the form $\frac{x}{a} = b$
- To recognize that a formula is a type of equation
- To solve equations containing fractions and mixed numbers

Words You Know

From the lists of "Words to Learn," choose the word or phrase that best completes each statement.

1. A sentence that contains an equal sign is a(n) _____.

2. An equation that contains a variable is called a(n) _____.

3. A number times its _____ equals 1.

4. A(n) _____ is an expression that states that two _____ are equal.

5. A value of a variable that makes an open sentence true is a(n) _____.

More Practice

State whether each equation is *true, false,* or *open.*

6. $14 = \frac{4}{5}y$ _____

7. $6 + 8 \div 2 = 7$ _____

8. $8 - (7 - 6) = 7$ _____

9. $3\frac{2}{3} + v = 5\frac{1}{6}$ _____

Which of the given values is the solution to each equation?

10. $\frac{n}{2} = 8$; 10, 6, 4, 16 _____

11. $20 = x - 4$; 16, 24, 5, 80 _____

Solve each equation by using mental math. Then check.

12. $p \div 5 = 7$ **13.** $15 = x + 7$

Substitute the values of the variables into the formula. Then solve the equation for the remaining variable.

14. $d = rt; d = 448, t = 7$ _____

15. $A = lw; A = 8, w = \frac{4}{3}$ _____

16. $s = r - d; s = 18, d = 3.75$ _____

Name the operation you can use to solve each equation.

17. $5 + h = 12$ _____

18. $\frac{7}{8} = 4t$ _____

Give the multiplicative inverse of each number.

19. $\frac{3}{8}$ _____   **20.** 24 _____

Solve each equation.

21. $p - 25 = 35$ **22.** $\frac{8}{9}k = 136$ **23.** $5\frac{4}{5} = 1\frac{3}{10} + x$

Problems You Can Solve

24. John uses $1\frac{1}{2}$ cups of milk and 3 cups of flour for his favorite cookie recipe. This makes 5 dozen cookies. Write and solve two proportions to see how much milk and flour he would need to make half as many cookies.

_____

_____

25. **For Your Portfolio**   For the next week, think about which of your activities could be described by an equation. Tripling the ingredients in a recipe would be one such activity. Finding your overtime income if you earn "time-and-a-half" for each hour worked overtime would be another. Write an equation for each activity. Exchange equations with a classmate. Then, solve each other's equations.

_____

_____

_____

Chapter 3   Practice Test

State whether each equation is *true, false*, or *open*.

1. $9 + 8 \div 2 = 13$ _____

2. $3.7 = y - 2.5$ _____

Which of the given values is the solution to the equation?

3. $4c = 12;\ 8,\ 48,\ 3,\ 16$ _____

Substitute the values of the variables into the formula. Then solve the equation for the remaining variable.

4. $A = lw;\ A = 75,\ l = 30$ _____

5. $s = r - d\ ;\ s = 49,\ d = 6$ _____

6. $d = rt\ ;\ d = 8.125,\ r = 3.25$ _____

Name the operation you can use to solve each equation.

7. $\frac{e}{8} = 21$ _____

8. $a - 13 = 14$ _____

Give the multiplicative inverse of each number.

9. 8 _____

10. $\frac{5}{9}$ _____

11. 1 _____

12. $3\frac{1}{4}$ _____

Solve each equation.

13. $5t = 30$

14. $k + \frac{5}{6} = 2\frac{3}{4}$

15. $12 = \frac{1}{6}n$

16. $c - 8.7 = 19.5$

17. $\frac{h}{14} = 15$

18. $\frac{7}{8}b = 231$

19. Louis saved enough money to buy a used car. If he paid a $600 deposit and still owes $1,200 that he must pay off in 12 months, what was the car's original price (p)? Write and solve an equation describing the situation.

_____

20. Louis drives too fast. In a 30-mile-per-hour speed zone, he drove 20 miles in $\frac{4}{9}$ hour (about 27 minutes).

   a. Write the formula you can use to find Louis's average speed. _____

   b. Substitute the values of the variables into the formula.
   _____

   c. Solve the equation to find Louis's average speed.
   _____

Chapter 4
Integers

OBJECTIVES:

In this chapter, you will learn
- *To recognize, use, compare, and order integers*
- *To locate an integer on a number line*
- *To use the absolute value of a number*
- *To add, subtract, multiply, and divide integers*

You have been working with positive numbers, numbers with values greater than zero. This chapter begins your study of negative numbers, numbers with values less than zero.

The chart below indicates the temperature ranges at which car motor oils will flow freely. Notice that the bar for 10W-30 oil indicates that the oil will flow freely when the temperature ranges from a low of 10°F below zero (−10°) to a high of 90°F above zero (+90°).

Which motor oil should you use in your car if the temperature where you live goes as low as −20° in the winter? What do you think the arrow on the bar for 5W-30 indicates?

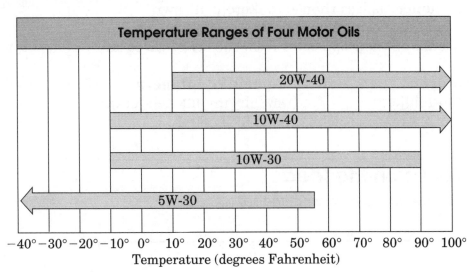

Temperature Ranges of Four Motor Oils

20W-40

10W-40

10W-30

5W-30

−40° −30° −20° −10° 0° 10° 20° 30° 40° 50° 60° 70° 80° 90° 100°
Temperature (degrees Fahrenheit)

◄4•1 What Is an Integer?

◄ IN THIS LESSON, YOU WILL LEARN

To recognize and use integers

WORDS TO LEARN

Whole numbers *numbers in the set {0, 1, 2, 3, 4,...}*

Opposites *two numbers that are the same distance from zero on a number line, but in opposite directions*

Integers *numbers in the set consisting of all whole numbers and their opposites {...,−2, −1, 0, 1, 2, 3,...}*

Negative integers *integers less than zero*

Positive integers *integers greater than zero*

Notice how the following sentences express mathematical opposites.

Statement:
Lamar's weight increased 10 pounds.
The elevator went up 5 floors.
The Eagles won 9 games.

Opposite:
Lamar's weight decreased 10 pounds.
The elevator went down 5 floors.
The Eagles lost 9 games.

New Idea

Whole numbers (hohl NUM-bers) are the numbers in the set {0, 1, 2, 3, ...}. Three dots (...) mean that the numbers continue on without stopping. Every whole number greater than zero is positive. A whole number, like seven, can be written as +7. Usually the plus sign is not written. So, a number without a sign is positive.

All integers have **opposites** (AWP-puh-sihts). Two numbers are opposites if they are the same distance from zero, but in opposite directions on a number line. The opposite of 7 is −7, which is read "negative seven." The negative sign (−) in front of a number means that the value of the number is less than zero. Zero is its own opposite, and zero is neither positive nor negative.

The whole numbers and their opposites form the set of **integers** (IHN-teh-jers).

negative integers	zero	**positive integers**
(NEHG-uh-tihv IHN-teh-jers)		(PAWS-ih-tihv IHN-teh-jers)
...,−4, −3, −2, −1	0	1, 2, 3, 4,...

◄ Focus on the Idea

An integer is a number in the set {..., −3, −2, −1, 0, 1, 2, 3,...}.

Practice

Write a statement that expresses the opposite of the given statement. The first one is done for you.

1. The quarterback gained 4 yards. _The quarterback lost 4 yards._

2. The temperature is 13 degrees below zero.

   _____

3. The price of CDs went up $1.50. _____

4. The balloon rose 250 feet. _____

5. Len saved $200 during April. _____

Write the opposite of the given integer.

6. 3 _____   7. -6 _____

8. -400 _____   9. positive 15 _____

10. negative 2 _____   11. the opposite of 20 _____

Describe a situation each integer could represent.

12. 20 _____

13. -35 _____

14. 0 _____

Apply the Idea

Write an integer to represent the distance above or below sea level. Explain how you decided whether the integer should be positive or negative.

15. The top of the World Trade Center is 1,400 feet above sea level. _____

16. The Puerto Rico Trench in the Atlantic Ocean is 28,232 feet below sea level. _____

Write About It

17. Scuba divers wear air tanks so that they can remain underwater. Do some research on scuba diving. Find out how far under water an experienced scuba diver can go safely. Use negative integers to write about your findings.

   _____

   _____

Integers and the Number Line

You can think of this thermometer as a vertical number line. It measures temperatures in degrees Fahrenheit (°F). On this scale, water boils at 212°F, comfortable room temperature is 68°F, and water freezes at 32°F.

Winter temperatures sometimes fall *below* 0°F. The lowest temperature ever recorded in Chicago, Illinois, was −27°F.

New Idea

A diagram with numbers shown as points is a **number line** (NUM-buhr lyen). On a horizontal number line, the numbers to the right of zero are positive. The numbers to the left of zero are negative. Integers are marked at evenly spaced points. Other points along the number line represent fractions and decimals.

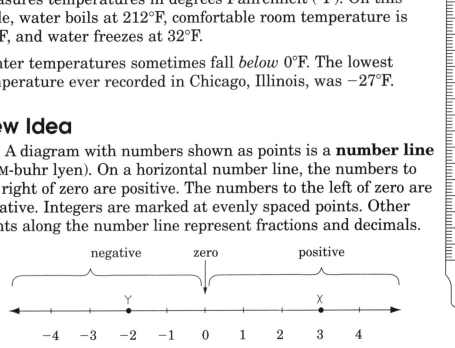

✓Check the Math

1. Hanna said she marked an X at 3 located on the number line above. Horatio said he marked a Y at negative 2. Are the letters at the correct places? How do you know?

▼## Focus on the Idea

On a horizontal number line, points to the left of zero represent negative numbers. Points to the right of zero represent positive numbers.

Practice

Write the number represented by the given letter. The first one is done for you.

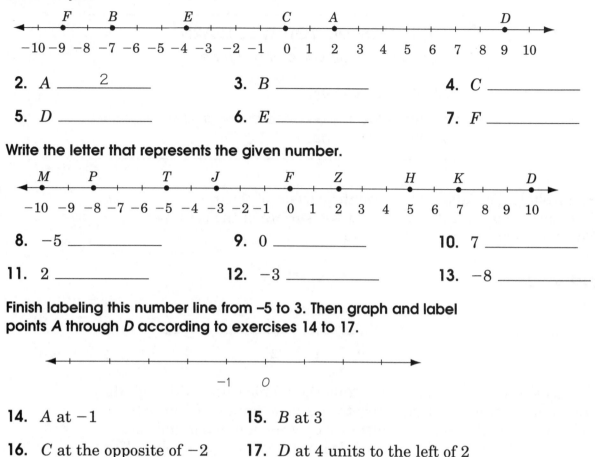

2. A ___2___

3. B _____

4. C _____

5. D _____

6. E _____

7. F _____

Write the letter that represents the given number.

8. -5 _____

9. 0 _____

10. 7 _____

11. 2 _____

12. -3 _____

13. -8 _____

Finish labeling this number line from −5 to 3. Then graph and label points *A* through *D* according to exercises 14 to 17.

14. A at -1

15. B at 3

16. C at the opposite of -2

17. D at 4 units to the left of 2

Apply the Idea

18. This thermometer measures temperatures in degrees Celsius (°C). On this scale, water boils at 100°C, normal body temperature is 37°C, comfortable room temperature is 20°C, water freezes at 0°C, and −10°C is the temperature on a very cold day. Label each of these temperatures on this thermometer.

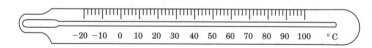

Write About It

19. Compare the Fahrenheit and Celsius thermometers. Which is a greater change in temperature, a change of 1°F or 1°C? Explain your answer.

_____

_____

4•3 Absolute Value

IN THIS LESSON, YOU WILL LEARN

To use the absolute value of a number

WORDS TO LEARN

Absolute value *the distance between a number and zero on a number line*

An airplane flies 1,000 feet above the surface of the ocean.
A submarine dives 1,000 feet below the surface of the ocean.
How far is each from the surface?

New Idea

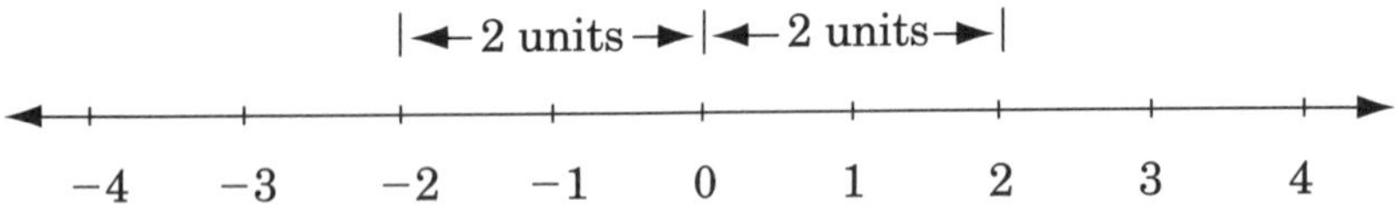

Look at the numbers 2 and −2 on the number line. Although they are different numbers, they are both the same number of units from zero on the number line. The distance between a number and zero is called the **absolute value** (ab-suh-loot VAL-yoo) of that number. The absolute value of a number may be either zero or a positive number. It may never be a negative number. To symbolize the absolute value of a number, you write the number between two small vertical lines.

Write: $|2| = 2$ Say: "The absolute value of two is two."

Write: $|-2| = 2$ Say: "The absolute value of negative two is two."

Another way to think about the absolute value of a number is as its numerical value without regard to its sign. In the problem at the beginning of the lesson, the plane flies at an altitude of 1,000 feet above the ocean's surface and the submarine dives to a depth of 1,000 feet below the surface. Both are 1,000 feet from the ocean's surface, but in opposite directions. Yet they represent the same absolute value.

$|1{,}000| = 1{,}000$ $|-1{,}000| = 1{,}000$

✓Check the Math

1. Can the absolute value of a number ever be equal to the opposite of that number? Explain.

▶ Focus on the Idea

The absolute value of a number is the distance between that number and zero.

Practice

$-10 \ -9 \ -8 \ -7 \ -6 \ -5 \ -4 \ -3 \ -2 \ -1 \quad 0 \quad 1 \quad 2 \quad 3 \quad 4 \quad 5 \quad 6 \quad 7 \quad 8 \quad 9 \quad 10$

Find the distance between the number and zero. The first one is done for you.

2. 4 _____4_____

3. −3 _____

4. −6 _____

5. 0 _____

6. 8 _____

7. −10 _____

Find each absolute value.

8. $|7|$ _____

9. $|-5|$ _____

10. $|-18|$ _____

11. $|-4\frac{1}{2}|$ _____

12. $|19.6|$ _____

13. $|-2.7|$ _____

Simplify each expression. The first one is done for you.

14. $|5| + |-2|$ _____7_____

15. $|-8| - |3|$ _____

16. $|-9| + |9|$ _____

17. $|-13| - |-4|$ _____

18. $5(|-3| + |4|)$ _____

19. $7(|-12| - |3|)$ _____

Apply the Idea

20. At 2 P.M., the temperature reached the high for the day, 13°F. Ten hours later, the temperature reached the low for the day. If the day's low had the same absolute value as the day's high, what was the temperature at midnight? _____

21. At 1 A.M., the temperature reached the low for the day, −3°F. Fourteen hours later, the temperature reached the high for the day. If the absolute value of the day's high was 19° higher than the absolute value of the day's low, what was the temperature at 3 P.M.? _____

✏ Write About It

22. A helicopter flies at an altitude of 1,220 feet above the ocean's surface. A submarine dives to a depth of 1,450 feet below the ocean's surface. Which is farther from the ocean's surface? Use absolute value to explain your answer.

_____

_____

_____

⬛4•4 Which Integer Is Greater?

City	Growth
Atlanta	−7%
Miami	+3%
Philadelphia	−5%
San Diego	+6%

This table lists the rates of growth in population in four United States cities from 1980 to 1990. Which city had a greater rate of growth, Miami or Philadelphia?

New Idea

You can use a number line to compare numbers. For any two numbers on a horizontal number line, the number farther to the right is the greater number. To compare the population growth rates of Miami and Philadelphia, compare 3 and −5.

Since 3 is farther to the right, 3 is greater than −5.

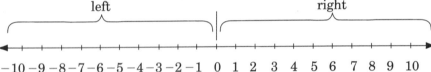

A statement that indicates that two numbers are *not* equal is called an **inequality** (ihn-ee-KWAWL-uh-tee). You can use one of the symbols shown here to write an inequality.

Write: $3 > -5$ Say: "Three is greater than negative five."
Write: $-5 < 3$ Say: "Negative five is less than three."

> **Inequality Symbols**
> $<$ means "less than"
> $>$ means "greater than"

✓Check Your Understanding

1. Use the information in the population growth chart. List the cities in order from greatest percent of growth to least percent of growth.

⬛Focus on the Idea

On a number line, the number farther to the right is the greater number. The number farther to the left is the lesser number.

Practice

Write the greater number for each pair. The first one is done for you.

2. 6 or 3 _____6_____ **3.** -7 or 7 _____

4. 0 or -1 _____ **5.** -3 or -4 _____

Write $<$, $>$, or $=$ in each ☐ .

6. -2 ☐ 1 **7.** 9 ☐ 13

8. -10 ☐ 0 **9.** 14 ☐ -18

10. -1.5 ☐ -2.4 **11.** $-2\frac{1}{2}$ ☐ $2\frac{1}{4}$

12. $|-4|$ ☐ $|3|$ **13.** $|24|$ ☐ $|-24|$

Write the integers in order, from least to greatest.

14. $\{3, -4, -2\}$ _____ **15.** $\{7, -8, 5\}$ _____

16. $\{-6, -9, -3\}$ _____ **17.** $\{1, -1, 0, -2\}$ _____

18. $\{-1, 7, -2, 5\}$ _____ **19.** $\{-20, 14, -23, -14\}$ _____

20. Find all the integer values of x that make $|x| < 4$ a true statement. _____

21. Use inequality symbols to compare -5 and 4 in two ways.

_____

Apply the Idea

22. In 1993, the Ferguson Equipment Company had a loss of $9,000,000. In 1994, the company's loss was $5,000,000. In which year did the company lose less money? Write an inequality that compares the two losses.

_____

Write About It

23. Write an inequality using two integers. Then write a word problem about a situation that can be described by that inequality.

_____

_____

_____

◢4•5 Adding Integers

IN THIS LESSON, YOU WILL LEARN

To add integers

WORDS TO LEARN

Sign *an indication that a number is left (−) or right (+) of zero on the number line*

Scott has a job parking cars at a garage. The garage has levels both above and below ground. Scott drives up to the third level to park a customer's car. He then takes the elevator down six levels to pick up another customer's car. Where is he now in relation to ground level?

Level 4
Level 3
Level 2
Level 1
Ground level
Basement 1
Basement 2
Basement 3
Basement 4

New Idea

You know how to add whole numbers. You can use this knowledge and a number line to add integers. Always start at 0. On a horizontal number line, add any positive integers by moving right. Add any negative integers by moving left.

Examples: Add. $-4 + (-2)$

Begin at 0 on the horizontal number line. Move left 4 units. Then move left 2 more units.

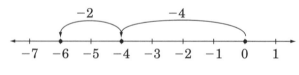

$-4 + (-2) = -6$

A vertical number line models Scott's garage. Use it to help you find Scott's location.

Add. $3 + (-6)$

Begin at 0 on the vertical number line. Move up 3 units. Then move down 6 units. $3 + (-6) = -3$. This shows that Scott is now in Basement 3.

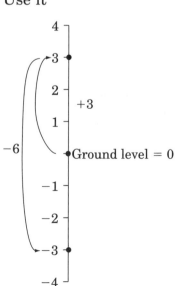

1. Draw arrows to help you find the sum of $-3 + 5$. What is the sum?

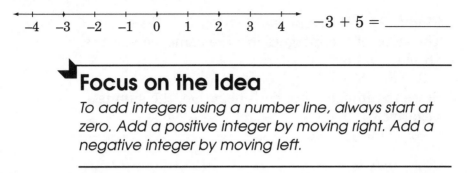

$-3 + 5 =$ _____

Focus on the Idea

To add integers using a number line, always start at zero. Add a positive integer by moving right. Add a negative integer by moving left.

Practice

Write the numbers that are being added on the number line. Then find the sum. The first one is done for you.

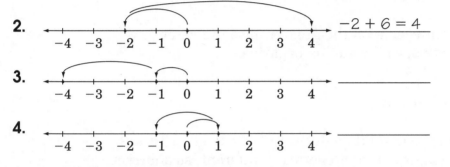

2. $-2 + 6 = 4$

3.   _____

4.   _____

Label a number line for each exercise. Then show the addition on the number line. Always begin at 0.

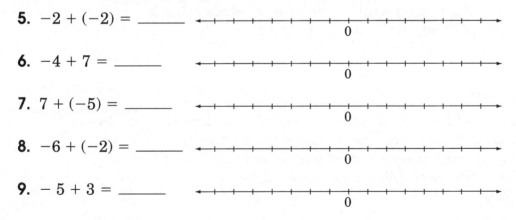

5. $-2 + (-2) =$ _____

6. $-4 + 7 =$ _____

7. $7 + (-5) =$ _____

8. $-6 + (-2) =$ _____

9. $-5 + 3 =$ _____

Extend the Idea

You have seen how to add integers using a number line. Another way to add integers is by following these rules:

- To add two integers with the *same* **sign** (syen), add their absolute values. The sign indicates that a number is left or right of zero on the number line. Give the sum the sign of the two integers.

- To add two integers with *different* signs, subtract their absolute values. Give the sum the sign of the integer with the greater absolute value.

Examples: Add. $-3 + (-5)$

Find the absolute values. $|-3| = 3 \qquad |-5| = 5$
The signs of the integers are the same, so add the absolute values.
  $3 + 5 = 8$
Since the integers are both negative, the sum is negative.
  $-3 + (-5) = -8$

Add. $-7 + 4$

Find the absolute values. $|-7| = 7 \qquad |4| = 4$
The signs of the integers are different, so subtract the absolute values.
  $7 - 4 = 3$
The integer with the greater absolute value is negative, so the sum is negative.
  $-7 + 4 = -3$

Add. $-2 + 9$

Find the absolute values. $|-2| = 2 \qquad |9| = 9$
The signs of the integers are different, so subtract the absolute values.
  $9 - 2 = 7$
The integer with the greater absolute value is positive, so the sum is positive.
  $-2 + 9 = 7$

✓Check the Math

10. Simon said he could check his answers to his integer sums by thinking of a number line. To check the answer to $-5 + (-8)$, Simon started at zero, moved 5 units to the left, and then 8 units to the right. Did Simon arrive at the correct answer? Explain.

_____

_____

Practice

Write whether you would *add* or *subtract* the absolute values of the integers to find the sum.

11. $5 + 6$ _____

12. $-8 + 2$ _____

13. $12 + (-10)$ _____ **14.** $-4 + (-9)$ _____

Find each sum.

15. $-5 + 6 =$ _____ **16.** $-3 + (-9) =$ _____

17. $7 + (-8) =$ _____ **18.** $-8 + 8 =$ _____

19. $-7 + (-8) =$ _____ **20.** $9 + 20 =$ _____

21. $8 + (-12) =$ _____ **22.** $-11 + (-13) =$ _____

23. $-6 + 13 =$ _____ **24.** $-15 + 18 =$ _____

25. $-13 + 1 =$ _____ **26.** $23 + (-16) =$ _____

Apply the Idea

27. Scott gets into a car at the ground level and drives to the fourth underground level. He then takes the elevator up three levels. What integer describes where Scott is in relation to the ground level?

_____

28. Scott drives from the ground level to the fourth level above ground. He takes the elevator down three levels. Then he drives a car down four levels to the service center. What integer describes where the service center is in relation to the ground level?

_____

Write About It

29. Draw a vertical number line to represent the number of floors in a building you have visited. It can be an apartment building, a department store, or an office building. Then write a word problem about that building that involves adding integers and has -3 as its answer.

_____

_____

_____

◀4•6 Subtracting Integers

▶ **IN THIS LESSON, YOU WILL LEARN**

To subtract integers

WORDS TO LEARN

Revenue *the total income of a business or an organization*

In business, profit *(P)* is the difference between **revenue** (REHV-uh-noo) *(R)*, meaning total income, and costs *(C)*. This can be written using the formula $P = R - C$. If P represents a negative number, the amount is a loss, instead of a profit.

During one month, a veterinarian has revenue of $3,400 and costs of $4,200. Does the veterinarian have a profit or a loss? What is the amount of profit or loss?

New Idea

To subtract integers, you can use the following rule: to subtract an integer, add its opposite.

According to the rule, you can rewrite a subtraction exercise as an addition exercise. Then, instead of subtracting the number, add its opposite.

Examples: Subtract. $-4 - 5$

Instead of subtracting 5, add the opposite of 5, which is -5.
$$-4 - 5 = -4 + (-5)$$
The integers have the same sign. Add the absolute values and give the sum the sign of the two integers.
$$|-4| + |-5| = 9, \text{ so } -4 - 5 = -9$$

Subtract. $-5 - (-8)$

Instead of subtracting -8, add the opposite of -8, which is 8.
$$-5 - (-8) = -5 + 8$$
The integers have different signs. Subtract the absolute values. The integer with the greater absolute value is positive, so the sum is positive.
$$-5 + 8 = 3$$

To find the veterinarian's profit or loss, subtract.
    3,400 − 4,200
Add the opposite of 4,200. Subtract absolute values.
    3,400 + (−4,200) = −800
The veterinarian's loss is $800.

Focus on the Idea
To subtract an integer, add its opposite.

Practice

Rewrite each subtraction as addition. The first one is done for you.

1. 6 − 10 $\underline{\quad 6 + (-10) \quad}$

2. −4 − (−3) _____

3. 8 − (−2)_____

4. −4 − 3 _____

Find each difference.

5. 4 − 7 = _____

6. 8 − (−3) = _____

7. −6 −(5) = _____

8. 3 − (−12) = _____

9. −7 − 8 = _____

10. −24 − 15 = _____

11. −43 − (−18) = _____

12. 36 − (−36) = _____

13. 100 −200 = _____

14. −48 − (−48) = _____

Complete each equation by writing the integer that makes it true.

15. 8 − _____ = 5

16. 8 − _____ = −5

17. 8 − _____ = 10

18. 8 − _____ = 20

Apply the Idea

19. Look back at the problem about the veterinarian. Suppose that, during the next month, the veterinarian has revenue of $5,900 and costs of $4,450. Will she have a profit or a loss? What will be the amount of profit or loss for the month?

_____

Write About It

20. Write a subtraction word problem that involves integers and has −4 as its answer.

_____

_____

_____

◤4•7 Multiplying Integers

Construction workers are digging a foundation for a skyscraper. They begin at sea level, where the **elevation** (ehl-uh-VAY-shuhn), or the distance above or below sea level, is at zero feet. (Above sea level, elevations are positive. Below sea level, elevations are negative.) Each day, they dig 9 feet deeper into the earth. What is their depth after 5 days?

New Idea

Recall that you can think of multiplication as repeated addition.

$$5 \cdot 9 = 9 + 9 + 9 + 9 + 9$$
$$= 45$$

Notice that the *product of two positive numbers is positive.*

You can also use repeated addition to multiply a positive integer by a negative integer.

$$5(-9) = (-9) + (-9) + (-9) + (-9) + (-9)$$
$$= (-18) + (-18) + (-9)$$
$$= (-36) + (-9)$$
$$= -45$$

Notice that the *product of a positive integer and a negative integer is negative.* The product, -45, tells you that after 5 days, the construction crew reaches a depth of -45 feet, or 45 feet below sea level.

Look for a pattern in these products:

$$(-3)3 = -9$$
$$(-3)2 = -6$$
$$(-3)1 = -3$$
$$(-3)0 = 0$$
$$(-3)(-1) = ?$$

The pattern of products suggests that $(-3)(-1) = 3$. Notice that (-3) and (-1) are both negative integers, so the *product of two negative integers is positive.*

The following rules summarize what you have learned.

- If two integers have the *same* sign, their product is positive.
- If two integers have *different* signs, their product is negative.

Focus on the Idea

When multiplying two integers, look at their signs. If the signs are the same, the product is positive. If the signs are different, the product is negative.

Practice

Write *positive* or *negative* for each product. Do not multiply. The first one is done for you.

1. $4(-6)$ ___negative___

2. $(-3)(-7)$ _____

3. $9 \cdot 12$ _____

4. $(-8)10$ _____

Find each product.

5. $3(-6) = $ _____

6. $(-4)(-4) = $ _____

7. $9 \cdot 7 = $ _____

8. $0(-7) = $ _____

9. $10 \cdot 8 = $ _____

10. $(-14)(-6) = $ _____

11. $32(-15) = $ _____

12. $(-5.8)(2.7) = $ _____

13. $(-2)(-2)(-2) = $ _____

14. $(-\frac{3}{4})(-1\frac{1}{4}) = $ _____

15. $(-1)(-2)(-3)(-4)(-5) = $ _____

16. $9(-3)(-5)(2)(-2) = $ _____

17. Find two integers whose sum is -9 and whose product is 20.

_____

Apply the Idea

18. A submarine descended from the surface of the ocean at a rate of 70 feet per minute. Find the depth of the submarine after 14 minutes. _____

Write About It

19. A negative number is multiplied by itself several times. Explain how to decide whether the final product is positive or negative.

_____

_____

_____

▶4•8 Dividing Integers

WORDS TO LEARN

Integers *numbers in the set consisting of all whole numbers and their opposites {. . . , –2, – 1, 0, 1, 2, 3. . .}*

Deep Sea Industries conducts underwater diving operations to recover the contents of wrecked ships. A diver descended to -96 feet to recover machine parts from a wrecked fishing boat. The descent took 3 minutes. Find the diver's rate of descent, or how many feet the diver descended per minute.

New Idea

Division and multiplication are inverse operations. This means that a multiplication sentence can be rewritten as a division sentence.

$$4 \cdot 3 = 12 \rightarrow 12 \div 3 = 4$$

You can use this fact to find rules for dividing two **integers**. (See Lesson 4•1.) Here are some related multiplication and division sentences. Look for patterns in the signs of the integers in the division column.

Multiplication		*Division*
$(2)(9) = 18$	$\longleftrightarrow$	$18 \div 9 = 2$
$(-2)9 = -18$	$\longleftrightarrow$	$(-18) \div 9 = -2$
$2(-9) = -18$	$\longleftrightarrow$	$(-18) \div (-9) = 2$
$(-2)(-9) = 18$	$\longleftrightarrow$	$18 \div (-9) = -2$

These examples illustrate two rules for dividing integers:
- If two integers have the *same* sign, their quotient is positive.
- If two integers have *different* signs, their quotient is negative.

You can find the diver's rate of descent by dividing -96 by 3.

$$\frac{-96}{3} = -32$$

The diver's rate of descent was 32 feet per minute.

▶Focus on the Idea

When dividing two integers, look at their signs. If the signs are the same, the quotient is positive. If the signs are different, the quotient is negative.

Practice

Write *positive* or *negative* for each quotient. Do not divide. The first one is done for you.

1. $14 \div (-2)$ ___negative___

2. $(-25) \div (-5)$ _____

3. $(-16) \div 4$ _____

4. $42 \div 7$ _____

Find each quotient.

5. $15 \div (-3) =$ _____

6. $(-30) \div 6 =$ _____

7. $20 \div 10 =$ _____

8. $49 \div (-7) =$ _____

9. $(-24) \div (-8) =$ _____

10. $44 \div (-11) =$ _____

11. $54 \div 9 =$ _____

12. $(-56) \div (-8) =$ _____

13. $8.0 \div (-1.6) =$ _____

14. $192 \div (-16) =$ _____

15. $182 \div 13 =$ _____

16. $(-224) \div 32 =$ _____

Complete each equation by writing the integer that makes it true.

17. $(-12) \div$ _____ $= -4$

18. _____ $\div 6 = 3$

19. _____ $\div (-2) = 15$

20. $45 \div$ _____ $= -9$

Apply the Idea

21. Over a 6-hour period, the outdoor temperature fell from $-3°F$ to $-21°F$.

   a. Calculate $-21 - (-3)$ to find the change in temperature over the entire period. _____

   b. Find the temperature change per hour. _____

22. Over a 3-hour period, temperature rose from $-10°C$ to $-4°C$.

   a. Find the change in temperature over the entire period.

   _____

   b. Find the temperature change per hour. _____

   c. If the temperature continues to rise at this rate, how many more hours will it be before it reaches the freezing point $(0°C)$? _____

Write About It

23. Marsha says that $0 \div 8 = 0$. Ted says that $0 \div 8 = 8$. Karen says that 0 cannot be divided by 8. Who is right? Explain.

_____

_____

Chapter 4 Review

In This Chapter, You Have Learned
- To recognize and use integers
- To locate an integer on a number line
- To use the absolute value of a number
- To compare and order integers
- To add, subtract, multiply, and divide integers

Words You Know

Write the letter of the entry in column 2 that best matches each word or phrase in column 1.

Column 1

1. absolute value _____

2. inequality _____

3. integers _____

4. negative integers _____

5. number line _____

6. opposites _____

7. positive integers _____

8. whole numbers _____

Column 2

a. $\{-1, -2, -3, -4, \ldots\}$

b. $-3 < 2$

c. -7 and 7, 5 and -5, 0 and 0

d.
$$\begin{array}{ccccccc} & & & & & & \\ \hline -2 & -1 & 0 & 1 & 2 & 3 & 4 \end{array}$$

e. $\{0, 1, 2, 3, \ldots\}$

f. $\{1, 2, 3, 4, \ldots\}$

g. $|-7| = 7$, $|4| = 4$

h. $\{\ldots, -4, -3, -2, -1, 0, 1, 2, \ldots\}$

More Practice

9. Write the opposite of -23. _____

Write the number represented by the letter above the number line.

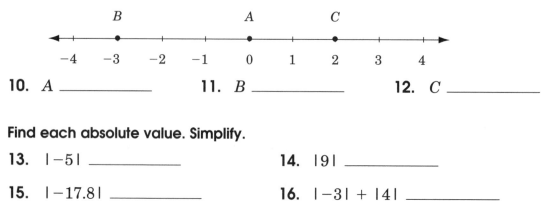

10. A _____   11. B _____   12. C _____

Find each absolute value. Simplify.

13. $|-5|$ _____   14. $|9|$ _____

15. $|-17.8|$ _____   16. $|-3| + |4|$ _____

Mark each point on the number line. Write the letter above the point.

17. A at -5 **18.** B at 3   **19.** C at 0

Write the numbers in order, from least to greatest.

20. $\{6, -6, -3, 3\}$ _____

21. $\{1, -1, -2, 0, -5, -8\}$ _____

Find each sum, difference, product, or quotient.

22. $(-5) + 7 = $ _____   **23.** $(-12) - 5 = $ _____

24. $(-14) \div (-2) = $ _____   **25.** $(-8)9 = $ _____

26. $(-6) + (-5) = $ _____   **27.** $13 - (-4) = $ _____

28. $(-20)(-20) = $ _____   **29.** $(-22) + 15 = $ _____

30. $(-48) \div 12 = $ _____   **31.** $45 - 50 = $ _____

Write $>$, $<$, or $=$ to make a true equation or inequality.

32. $16 + (-20)$ _____ $12 \div (-3)$ **33.** $(-3)7$ _____ $(-30) - (-10)$

34. $(-15) \div 5$ _____ $8 - 12$ **35.** $-14 + 13$ _____ $6 \div (-3)$

Problems You Can Solve

36. A diving platform is 10 feet above the surface of the water. Don dives a total of 22 feet from the platform to the deepest point in his dive. What depth does Don reach? _____

37. Sally's checking account statement has an entry of $-80¢$. This entry is a fee for processing 4 checks. What is the fee per check? _____

38. **For Your Portfolio**   Create "The Game of Integers." The game should begin with a group of students sitting in a circle. Write a paragraph explaining the game. Be sure to state the rules. Tell what students may learn from the game.

_____

_____

_____

Chapter 4   Practice Test

1. Write the opposite of 15. _____

Use the number line to complete exercises 2 and 3.

2. Write the number represented by point P. _____
3. Mark the -3 point on the number line and write the letter Q above it.

Find each absolute value. Simplify.

4. $|-13|$ _____   5. $|7|$ _____

6. $|-9| + |-5|$ _____   7. $|5| + |-5|$ _____

8. $|-9 + (-5)|$ _____   9. $|5 + (-5)|$ _____

Write the numbers in order, from least to greatest.

10. $\{4, 0, -3, -1\}$ _____

11. $\{5, -1, 1, -5, 0\}$ _____

Find each sum, difference, product, or quotient.

12. $7 - (-2) =$ _____   13. $(-4)(-7) =$ _____

14. $(-3) + 2 =$ _____   15. $21 \div 7 =$ _____

16. $15 + (-10) =$ _____ 17. $8(-5) =$ _____

18. $(-9) \div (-3) =$ _____ 19. $(-13) - 15 =$ _____

20. $(-16)4 =$ _____   21. $(-8) - (-3) =$ _____

22. $0 + (-9) =$ _____   23. $45 \div (-9) =$ _____

Write $>$, $<$, or $=$ to make a true equation or inequality.

24. $9 - 14$ _____ $(-7) - 2$

25. $6(-2)$ _____ $(-20) \div 2$

Chapter 5

Introduction to Graphing

OBJECTIVES:

In this chapter, you will learn

- *To name the parts of a coordinate plane*
- *To locate points on a coordinate plane*
- *To use and graph a table of x- and y-values*
- *To recognize a graph that is horizontal or vertical*
- *To find the slope of a line*
- *To find the x-intercept and y-intercept of a line*

Nutritional Values of Four Foods

	Milk 1 c	Peach 1 small	Almonds 1 c	Lentils 1 c
Calories	150	37	849	212
Protein	8 g	1 g	26 g	16 g
Carbohydrates	11 g	10 g	28 g	39 g

How much protein is in one cup of almonds?

The skills you use to read data from a table are like skills you use in graphing. Each number in the table is at the point where a column and a row meet. To find the protein in one cup of almonds, you look for the point where the "almonds" column and the "protein" row meet. There are 26 grams of protein in one cup of almonds.

In this chapter, you will use a similar method to locate points on a coordinate plane.

5•1 The Coordinate Plane

WORDS TO LEARN

Axes *two perpendicular number lines that meet at their zero points*

Coordinates *the two numbers used to locate a point on a coordinate plane*

Coordinate plane *a region formed by a pair of axes*

Quadrants *the four regions into which a coordinate plane is divided; the axes are not part of the quadrants*

One way to show a location on a map is to use a letter and a number to indicate each *region*. On this map of New Mexico, the city of Roswell is located in region E3.

New Idea

Another way to show a location is to use two numbers to indicate a *point* on the map. This map shows a city in which 0 Street and 0 Avenue are two **axes** (AK-seez) that meet at right angles at the center of town. North and south of 0 Street are numbered streets. East and west of 0 Avenue are numbered avenues. An address can be given by naming two **coordinates** (koh-AWR-duh-nihts)—one street and one avenue. The whole map is a kind of **coordinate plane** (koh-AWR-duh-niht playn). It is divided by 0 Street and 0 Avenue into four regions, or **quadrants** (KWAH-druhnts)—northeast (NE), northwest (NW), southwest (SW), and southeast (SE).

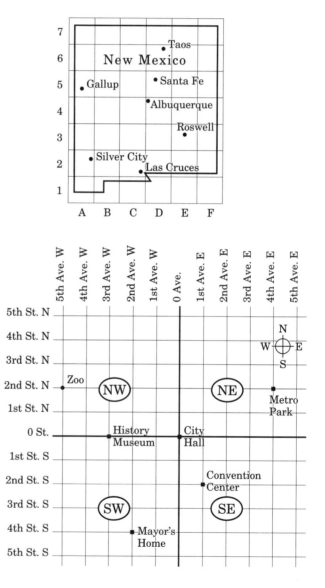

Example: What are the coordinates of the location of Metro Park?

Metro Park is at 4th Ave. East and 2nd Street North, or 4 east, 2 north.

◄ Focus on the Idea

Every number line has a single 0 point. Two number lines that meet at right angles at their 0 points form a coordinate plane. Any point in the plane can be located using two coordinates.

Practice

Refer to the map. Start at City Hall to find how many blocks and in which direction you must walk to get to each place. Give the east-west coordinate first. The first one is done for you.

1. Mayor's home <u>2 west, 4 south</u>   2. Zoo _____

3. History Museum _____   4. City Hall _____

Start at City Hall. Mark the location identified with a dot and a letter.

5. Write *A* at 4 east, 5 south.   6. Write *C* at 0 east or west, 3 north.

7. Write *B* at 4 west, 1 south.   8. Write *D* at 3 east, 0 north or south.

Name the quadrant in which each place or set of coordinates is located.

9. Zoo _____   10. Convention Center _____

11. 2 east, 2 north _____   12. 7 south, 8 west _____

Apply the Idea

Find the number of blocks between each pair of coordinates.

13. 3 east, 4 north and 3 east, 5 south _____

14. 11 west, 18 north and 11 west, 27 south _____

✎ Write About It

15. Write a paragraph telling why two coordinates are needed to locate a point on a coordinate plane.

_____

_____

René Descartes (1596–1650) was a gifted mathematician. One day, he saw a fly crawling on a tiled ceiling. He imagined that the tiles were a coordinate plane. Then, by naming just two numbers on the "plane," he could give the fly's location at any moment. We still use Descartes's basic idea to describe a point using two coordinates.

New Idea

In mathematics, a coordinate plane is identified by a pair of axes. The **x-axis** (EHKS-ak-sihs) is a horizontal number line. The **y-axis** (WY-ak-sihs) is a vertical number line. As the figure shows, the two axes meet at right angles at their zero points. The point at which they meet is called the **origin** (OHR-ih-jihn). The axes divide the plane into four quadrants, numbered I, II, III, and IV.

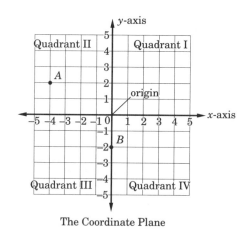

The Coordinate Plane

The **x-coordinate** (EHKS-koh-AWR-duh-niht) (x) tells the number of units right or left of the origin. The **y-coordinate** (WY-koh-AWR-duh-niht) (y) tells the number of units up or down from the origin. Together, the coordinates form an **ordered pair** (x, y) that tells where the point is located. Point A has coordinates $(-4, 2)$. Point B has coordinates $(0, -2)$. The origin has coordinates $(0, 0)$.

Remember

In an ordered pair, the x-coordinate always is listed first.

◀ Focus on the Idea

The ordered pair (x, y) gives the x-coordinate and the y-coordinate for a point.

Practice

Give the ordered pair for each point. The first one is done for you.

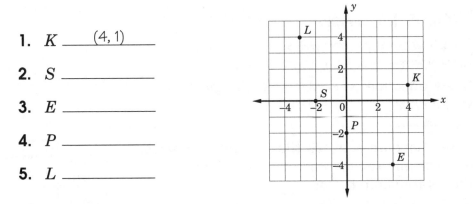

1. K ___(4, 1)___

2. S _____

3. E _____

4. P _____

5. L _____

On the graph above, draw a point to locate each ordered pair. Label it with the given letter.

6. $G\,(2, 5)$

7. $N\,(-3, -2)$

8. $I\,(-3, 2)$

9. $W\,(-2, 3)$

10. $C\,(-3, 0)$

11. $T\,(0, -4)$

Name the quadrant in which the point for each ordered pair is located.

12. $(-2, 5)$ _____

13. $(1, -4)$ _____

14. $(-9, -13)$_____

Find the distance between the points for each pair of coordinates.

15. $(3, 5)$ and $(3, 1)$ _____

16. $(21, 24)$ and $(4, 24)$ _____

Apply the Idea

17. An airline map looks like a coordinate plane with a grid marked in miles. When at a point directly above $(-15, 18)$ on the map, a pilot receives directions from the ground. She is told to fly south 23 miles, then east 21 miles. What ordered pair describes the pilot's final position? _____

✎ Write About It

18. Is the point $(2, 5)$ on the coordinate plane the same as the point $(5, 2)$? Explain your answer.

_____

_____

5•3 Tables and Graphs

IN THIS LESSON, YOU WILL LEARN

To use an equation to make a table of x- and y-values

To graph a linear equation, using a table of values

WORDS TO LEARN

Graph of an equation *the set of points whose coordinates make an equation true*

Linear equation *an equation whose graph is a straight line*

This table shows the relationship between the amount of gasoline used by one late-model car and the distance it was driven. Can a graph show the relationship better?

Gas used (gal)	Distance (mi)
1	25
2	50
3	75
4	100
5	125
6	150

New Idea

You already have solved equations with one variable. Now you will learn to use equations with two variables. An equation with one variable has one solution. An equation with two variables has many solutions.

To draw a **graph of an equation** (graf, ee-KWAY-zhun) with two variables, find ordered pairs that make the equation true. Then plot a point for each ordered pair on a coordinate plane. Connect the points to show your graph.

Example: Graph the equation. $y = 2x - 3$

Choose at least three values of x, and substitute them into the equation $y = 2x - 3$. Then, for each value of x, solve for y.

x	y	(x, y)
−1	−5	(−1, −5)
2	1	(2, 1)
4	5	(4, 5)

If $x = -1$, then:
$$y = 2x - 3$$
$$y = 2(-1) - 3$$
$$y = -2 - 3$$
$$y = -5$$

If $x = 2$, then:
$$y = 2x - 3$$
$$y = 2(2) - 3$$
$$y = 4 - 3$$
$$y = 1$$

If $x = 4$, then:
$$y = 2x - 3$$
$$y = 2(4) - 3$$
$$y = 8 - 3$$
$$y = 5$$

A point for each ordered pair (x, y) is plotted on the coordinate plane shown here. The points are connected to create the graph. The graph is a straight line, so the equation $y = 2x - 3$ is called a **linear equation** (LIHN-ee-uhr ee-KWAY-zhuhn).

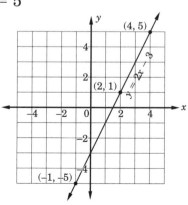

Focus on the Idea

To graph a linear equation, find and graph at least three ordered pairs (x, y) that make the equation true.

Practice

Use the equation $y = 3x + 4$. Find the value of y for each value of x given. The first one has been done for you.

1. $x = 1$ $y =$ ____7____

2. $x = 3$ $y =$ _____

3. $x = -2$ $y =$ _____

4. $x = 0$ $y =$ _____

For each equation, find the y-values and write the ordered pairs. Then draw the graph on the coordinate grid.

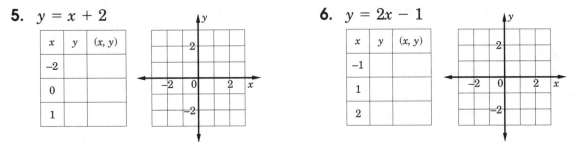

5. $y = x + 2$

x	y	(x, y)
-2		
0		
1		

6. $y = 2x - 1$

x	y	(x, y)
-1		
1		
2		

Apply the Idea

7. Use the gasoline mileage table on page 84.

   a. Sketch a graph for the amount of gas used and the distance driven.

   b. What do the points you graphed tell you about the amount of gas used and the distance driven?

   _____

   _____

Write About It

8. Look back at the graph of the equation $y = 2x - 3$ on page 84. Use the graph to help you solve the equation $2x - 3 = -1$. Then write a paragraph about the method you used.

   _____

   _____

   _____

◢5•4 Special Graphs

Crispy Rice cereal sells for $3 per box. Is the graph of this relationship a line?

Number of boxes	1	2	3	4	5
Cost (in dollars)	3	6	9	12	15

New Idea

The graph of the equation $y = x - 2$ is shown here. Every point on the line, even a point with coordinates that are fractions or decimals, represents a solution of the equation. Because you can draw the graph without taking your pencil off the page, it is called a **continuous graph** (kuhn-TIHN-yoo-uhs graf).

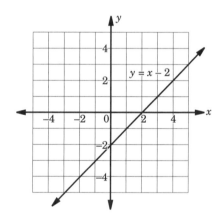

The graph that shows the relationship between Crispy Rice prices and cost is shown here. Because you can buy only whole boxes of cereal, and not fractional or decimal parts of a box, all the x- and y-coordinates for this graph are whole numbers. A graph with gaps in it is called a **discrete graph** (dih-SKREET graf).

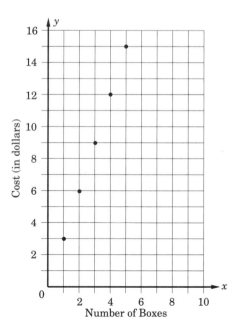

On the vertical line graphed here, every point has an x-coordinate of -2. The equation of the vertical line is $x = -2$. On the horizontal line graphed, every point has a y-coordinate of 4. The equation of the horizontal line is $y = 4$.

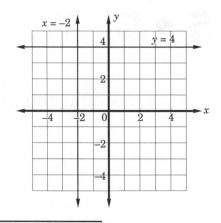

◣ Focus on the Idea

A graph may be continuous or discrete. Each point on the graph of a vertical line has the same x value. Each point on the graph of a horizontal line has the same y value.

Practice

Use the words *continuous, discrete, vertical,* **or** *horizontal* **to describe each graph. You may use more than one word. The first one is done for you.**

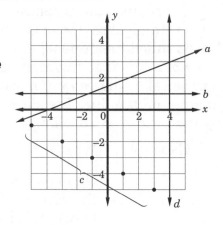

1. Graph a ____continuous____

2. Graph b _____

3. Graph c _____

4. Graph d _____

Write the equation.

5. A vertical line passes through the point $(-3, 5)$. What is the equation of the line? _____

6. A horizontal line passes through the point $(-4, -7)$. What is the equation of the line? _____

Apply the Idea

Tell if the graph would be *continuous, discrete, vertical,* **or** *horizontal.* **You may want to sketch a graph.**

7. A package of stove bolts weighs 2 ounces. Let x = number of packages. Let y = total weight of the packages. _____

8. Copper tubing weighs 3 ounces per inch. Let x = length of tubing. Let y = total weight of the tubing. _____

✎ Write About It

9. Where do the lines $x = 5$ and $y = -3$ intersect on a coordinate plane? Explain your answer.

_____

▶5•5 Slope

▶ **IN THIS LESSON, YOU WILL LEARN**

To find the slope of a line

WORDS TO LEARN

Slope *the measure of the steepness of a line*

The figure shows the bed of a dump truck in two different positions. In which position, A or B, does the truck bed have the steeper slope?

New Idea

Every line has steepness. Line n is steeper than line m. In algebra, the measure of the steepness of a line is called its **slope** (slohp). One way to find the slope of a line is to find the vertical change and the horizontal change as you move from one point to another on the line. The slope of a line is expressed by the ratio, vertical change to horizontal change.

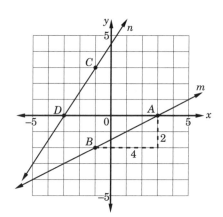

Example: What is the slope of line m?

On line m, as you move from A to B, the vertical change is 2. The horizontal change is 4.

$$\text{Slope} = \frac{\text{vertical change}}{\text{horizontal change}} = \frac{2}{4} = \frac{1}{2}$$

Here is another way to find the slope of a line. Start with two points on the line. Line p is the graph of $y = -\frac{2}{3}x + 1$. Two points on the line are $(0, 1)$ and $(3, -1)$.

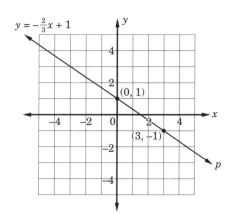

$$\text{Slope} = \frac{\text{change in } y}{\text{change in } x}$$

$$= \frac{1 - (-1)}{(0 - 3)} = \frac{2}{-3} = -\frac{2}{3}$$

Notice that the slope is the coefficient of x in the equation $y = -\frac{2}{3}x + 1$. When an equation is written in the form $y = mx + b$, where m and b represent numbers, m is the slope of the line.

✓Check Your Understanding

1. On line n above, move from point C to point D. What is the slope of line n? _____

Focus on the Idea

The slope of a line is its steepness. Slope can be expressed in two ways: $\frac{vertical\ change}{horizontal\ change}$ or $\frac{change\ in\ y}{change\ in\ x}$

Practice

Give the coordinates of the two graphed points. Then find the slope of the line containing the two points. The first one is done for you.

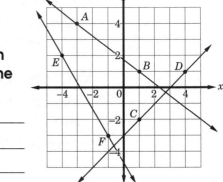

2. A ___(−3, 4)___ B ___(1, 1)___   slope ___$-\frac{3}{4}$___

3. C _____ D _____   slope _____

4. E _____ F _____   slope _____

Find the slope of the line that passes through each pair of points.

5. $(2, 3)$ and $(10, 7)$ _____

6. $(-2, -5)$ and $(4, 3)$_____

7. $(4, 0)$ and $(5, 9)$ _____

8. $(-1, -2)$ and $(2, -5)$ _____

Use any two ordered pairs that are solutions to the equation to find the slope of the graph of the line.

9. $y = 3x - 4$ _____

10. $y = -5x + 7$ _____

11. $y = -\frac{4}{7}x - 6$ _____

12. $y = -2$ _____

Apply the Idea

13. A gear on an assembly machine turns at the rate of $\frac{1}{2}$ revolution per second. Let x = time in seconds. Let y = number of revolutions. Graph the relationship and give the slope of the graph.

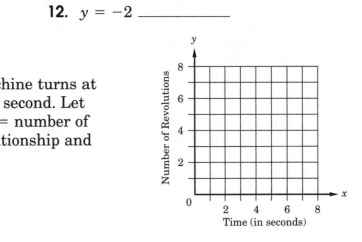

✍ Write About It

14. Look again at the graphed lines in this chapter. How do the lines differ? How can you tell if a line has a positive or a negative slope just by looking at the line?

_____

_____

_____

⬆5•6 Finding the Intercepts of an Equation

⬆ **IN THIS LESSON, YOU WILL LEARN**

To use a graph or an equation to find the x-intercept and y-intercept of a line

WORDS TO LEARN

x-intercept *the x-coordinate of the point where a line intersects the x-axis*

y-intercept *the y-coordinate of a point where a line intersects the y-axis*

A missile *intercepts* its target. A secret agent *intercepts* a coded message. A defensive back *intercepts* a pass. The word *intercepts* suggests that two things meet. A graphed line can intercept each coordinate axis.

New Idea

The line shown crosses the x-axis at $(3, 0)$. The x-coordinate of that point, 3, is called the **x-intercept** (ehks-IHN-tuhr-sept) of that line. The line crosses the y-axis at $(0, -2)$. The y-coordinate of that point, -2, is called the **y-intercept** (wy-IHN-tuhr-sept) of that line.

Notice that the x-intercept of the line has a y-coordinate of 0. The y-intercept of the line has an x-coordinate of 0. You can use the equation of a line to find the x- and y-intercepts of the line.

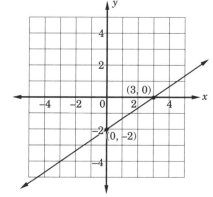

Example: Find the x- and y-intercepts of the graph of $y = x + 5$.

To find the x-intercept:

$y = x + 5$ ←Substitute 0 for y.

$0 = x + 5$ ←Solve for x.

$x = -5$

The x-intercept is -5.

To find the y-intercept:

$y = x + 5$ ←Substitute 0 for x.

$y = 0 + 5$ ←Solve for y.

$y = 5$

The y-intercept is 5.

⬆ Focus on the Idea

To find the x-intercept of a line, use a y-value of 0. To find the y-intercept of a line, use an x-value of 0.

Practice

Give the *x*-intercept and the *y*-intercept of each line. The first one has been done for you.

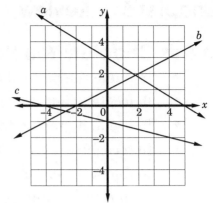

1. line *a* _____ x-intercept: 5, y-intercept: 3 _____

2. line *b* _____

3. line *c* _____

For each equation, find the *x*-intercept and the *y*-intercept of the graph.

4. $y = x + 4$ _____

5. $y = 2x - 6$ _____

6. $y = \frac{1}{2}x + 3$ _____

7. $y = 5x - 8$ _____

8. $4x - 3y = 12$ _____

9. $7x + 5y = 35$ _____

10. The *x*-intercept of a line is -8. Give the coordinates of the point where the line intersects the *x*-axis. _____

11. The *x*-intercept of the line with the equation $y = 2x + b$ is 20. Find the value of *b*. _____

12. Give the equation of a line with no *x*-intercept. _____

Apply the Idea

13. Both the Fahrenheit scale and the Celsius scale are used to measure temperature. The formula $F = \frac{9}{5}C + 32$ expresses the relationship between Celsius temperature (°C) and Fahrenheit temperature (°F).

    a. Find the Fahrenheit temperature for 0° Celsius. _____

    b. Find the Celsius temperature for 104° Fahrenheit. _____

    c. If you graphed the formula with *C* on the *x*-axis and *F* on the *y*-axis, what would be the slope of the graph and the *y*-intercept? _____

✐ Write About It

14. How can you use the *x*- and *y*-intercepts to graph an equation? Write a paragraph explaining your method.

    _____

    _____

    _____

    _____

Chapter 5   Review

In This Chapter, You Have Learned

- To name the parts of a coordinate plane
- To locate points on a coordinate plane
- To use and graph a table of x- and y-values
- To recognize a graph that is horizontal or vertical
- To find the slope of a line
- To find the x-intercept and y-intercept of a line

Words You Know

From the lists of "Words to Learn," choose the word or phrase that best completes each statement.

1. Two perpendicular number lines that meet at their zero points are called _____.

2. A(n) _____ can be drawn without lifting the pencil off the paper.

3. A region formed by a pair of axes is a(n) _____.

4. _____ are the two numbers used to locate a point on a coordinate plane.

5. The _____ is the set of points whose coordinates make an equation true.

6. An equation whose graph is a straight line is a(n) _____.

7. The point at which the x-axis and the y-axis meet at right angles is the _____.

More Practice

Refer to the bottom map on page 80. Find the number of blocks between each pair of coordinates.

8. 8 west, 3 north and 8 west, 17 north _____

9. 4 east, 10 south and 11 west, 10 south _____

Name the coordinates of each point on the graph at the right.

10. A _____   11. B _____   12. C _____

On the graph, draw and label each point.

13. $D\,(-4, 1)$ 14. $E\,(1, -5)$ 15. $F\,(2, 0)$

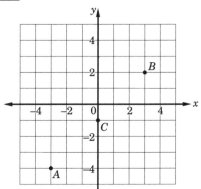

Name the quadrant in which each point is located.

16. $(3, -2)$ _____   **17.** $(-16, -19)$ _____

Find the distance between each pair of points.

18. $(6, -8)$ and $(6, -1)$ _____   **19.** $(-11, -6)$ and $(14, -6)$ _____

Use the equation $y = -3x + 5$. Find y for each given value of x.

20. $x = 2$, $y =$ _____   **21.** $x = -4.5$, $y =$ _____

22. Complete the table of values for the equation $y = 2x - 2$. Then sketch the graph of the equation.

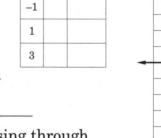

x	y	(x, y)
-1		
1		
3		

23. A vertical line passes through the point $(6, -1)$. What is the equation of the line? _____

24. Find the slope of the line passing through the points $(1, -3)$ and $(-1, 3)$. _____

Find the slope of the graph of each linear equation.

25. $y = 2x + 5$ _____   **26.** $3x - 12y = 2$ _____

Find the x-intercept and the y-intercept of the graph of each equation.

27. $y = x - 6$ _____   **28.** $4x - 7y = 28$ _____

Problems You Can Solve

29. If the slope of a ladder leaning against a wall is 4, and the base of the ladder is 3 feet from the wall, how far up the wall does the ladder reach? (Hint: Draw a diagram on graph paper to help.) _____

30. **For Your Portfolio**   Here is the game of "Slopes and Intercepts." Each player draws a line on a set of coordinate axes on a sheet of graph paper. Then the player writes his or her name below the graph. On a separate sheet, the player notes the slope and the two intercepts of the line. Players place their graphs where everyone can see them. Players figure out the slopes and intercepts of all but their own graphs. When this is done, each player reads the slope and intercepts of his or her graph. Other players check their answers, giving themselves 1 point for each correct answer. Players lose 1 point if they incorrectly identify the slopes or intercepts. Play a few rounds with some classmates. On a separate sheet of paper, write a paragraph about what happens.

Chapter 5   Practice Test

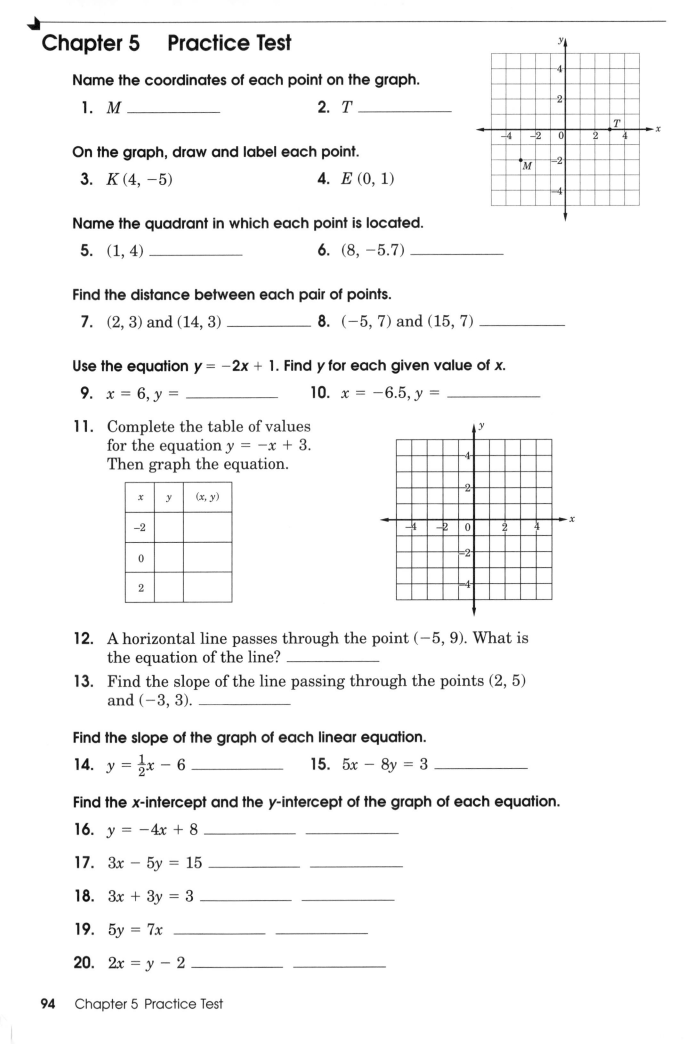

Name the coordinates of each point on the graph.

1. M _____

2. T _____

On the graph, draw and label each point.

3. $K\ (4, -5)$

4. $E\ (0, 1)$

Name the quadrant in which each point is located.

5. $(1, 4)$ _____

6. $(8, -5.7)$ _____

Find the distance between each pair of points.

7. $(2, 3)$ and $(14, 3)$ _____

8. $(-5, 7)$ and $(15, 7)$ _____

Use the equation $y = -2x + 1$. Find y for each given value of x.

9. $x = 6, y =$ _____

10. $x = -6.5, y =$ _____

11. Complete the table of values for the equation $y = -x + 3$. Then graph the equation.

x	y	(x, y)
-2		
0		
2		

12. A horizontal line passes through the point $(-5, 9)$. What is the equation of the line? _____

13. Find the slope of the line passing through the points $(2, 5)$ and $(-3, 3)$. _____

Find the slope of the graph of each linear equation.

14. $y = \frac{1}{2}x - 6$ _____

15. $5x - 8y = 3$ _____

Find the *x*-intercept and the *y*-intercept of the graph of each equation.

16. $y = -4x + 8$ _____ _____

17. $3x - 5y = 15$ _____ _____

18. $3x + 3y = 3$ _____ _____

19. $5y = 7x$ _____ _____

20. $2x = y - 2$ _____ _____

Chapter 6

More About Graphing

◢ OBJECTIVES:

In this chapter, you will learn

- *To identify and find rate of change*
- *To graph a linear equation using the slope and y-intercept*
- *To rewrite an equation in standard form*
- *To graph absolute-value equations*
- *To recognize the graphs of parallel lines and perpendicular lines*
- *To recognize the graph of one form of a quadratic equation*

1.

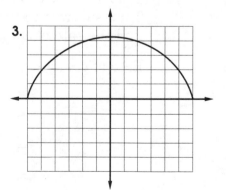

2.

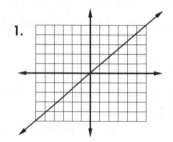

Graphs provide a kind of picture of the way real things look or behave. Graph 1 is a model of a linear equation. It represents the slope of the steepest street in the world, Baldwin Street in Dunedin, New Zealand.

3.

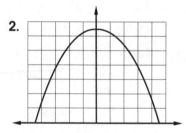

Architects use graphs to design buildings and other structures. Graph 2 is a model of the Gateway Arch in St. Louis.

Design engineers use graphs to study how products behave under extreme conditions. Graph 3 is a model of a baseball at the moment it is struck by a bat.

◀6•1 Slope as Rate of Change

◀ IN THIS LESSON, YOU WILL LEARN

To identify and find rate of change

WORDS TO LEARN

Rate *a ratio of two measurements expressed in different units.*

Rate of change *the ratio that expresses the change in one quantity in relation to the change in another quantity*

The Indianapolis 500 is a 500-mile auto race held each year on Memorial Day. The first race was in 1911. The winner, Ray Harroun, averaged 74.59 miles per hour. The race record was set in 1990 by Arie Luyendyk. He averaged 185.984 miles per hour.

New Idea

A **rate** (rayt) is a ratio of two measurements expressed in different units. Often, the word *per* is used to indicate a rate. Sometimes, a rate changes over time. A **rate of change** (rayt uhv chaynj) is the change in one quantity as compared with the change in another quantity.

The expression, 29 miles per gallon, is a rate because it describes two different units—miles and gallons. The expression means 1 gallon of fuel will transport a vehicle 29 miles.

Examples: What was the rate of change in average winning speeds at the Indianapolis 500 between 1911 and 1990?

The average winning speed changed from 74.59 miles per hour in 1911 to 185.984 miles per hour in 1990. Subtract to find the change in winning speeds. Then subtract to find the change in years. Divide to find the rate of change.

$$\text{Rate of change} = \frac{\text{Change in speeds}}{\text{Change in years}}$$

$$= \frac{185.984 - 74.59}{1990 - 1911} \quad \leftarrow \text{Subtract numerators and denominators.}$$

$$= \frac{111.394}{79} \quad \leftarrow \text{Divide.}$$

$$= 1.41 \text{ mi/h each year}$$

From 1911 to 1990, the winning speed changed by about 1.41 miles per hour each year.

Remember

The slope of a line is the ratio:

$$\frac{\text{Vertical change}}{\text{Horizontal change}} \quad \text{or} \quad \frac{\text{Change in } y}{\text{Change in } x}$$

The slope of the line shown is $\frac{4}{6}$, or $\frac{2}{3}$. Because slope is a ratio of the change in one quantity to the change in another, it is an example of rate of change.

Focus on the Idea

Rate of change compares changes in two quantities. The slope of a line is an example of a rate of change.

Practice

Find each rate of change. The first one is started for you.

1. Gasoline was $0.40 per gallon in 1970 and $1.15 per gallon in 1995. Find the rate of change in price per year.

   Rate of change $= \dfrac{\text{Change in price}}{\text{Change in years}} = \dfrac{\$1.15 - \$0.40}{1995 - 1970}$

   The rate of change in the price of gasoline was _____ per year.

2. A line passes through the points (3, 5) and (7, 13) on a coordinate grid.

   Slope $= \dfrac{\text{Vertical change}}{\text{Horizontal change}} = \dfrac{\text{Change in } y}{\text{Change in } x} = $ _____

3. A line passes through the points $(-4, 11)$ and $(1, -4)$. Find the slope. _____

4. Find the slope of the line that passes through the points $(7, 1)$ and $(0, -3)$. _____

Apply the Idea

5. The federal minimum hourly wage rate rose from $.75 per hour in 1950 to $4.25 in 1991. Find the yearly rate of change in the minimum wage to the nearest cent. _____

Write About It

6. Suppose you know how much a certain item cost in 1985 and the yearly rate of change in its cost. Explain how you could find how much the item cost in 1995.

   _____

   _____

6•2 Using the Slope-Intercept Form of an Equation

IN THIS LESSON, YOU WILL LEARN

To graph a linear equation using slope and y-intercept

To write a linear equation using slope and y-intercept

WORDS TO LEARN

Slope-intercept form *a linear equation written in the form $y = mx + b$*

The Americans with Disabilities Act, in effect since January 1992, states that all public buildings must be wheelchair accessible. A carpenter is building a ramp from a sidewalk to a doorway. If the slope of the ramp and the height of the doorway are known, can the carpenter calculate where on the sidewalk the ramp should begin?

New Idea

A linear equation written in the form $y = mx + b$ is said to be in **slope-intercept form** (slohp IHN-tuhr-sehpt fawrm). In this form, m stands for the slope of the line and b stands for the y-intercept, the point where the graph crosses the y-axis.

Examples: If the slope of a line is $\frac{1}{2}$ and the y-intercept is -4, what is the equation for the line?

Substitute $\frac{1}{2}$ for m and -4 for b in the equation $y = mx - b$.

$$y = \tfrac{1}{2}x + -4$$

Use the slope-intercept form to graph the equation $4y = 3x - 8$.

First, find the slope and the y-intercept.

$$4y = 3x - 8$$

$$\frac{4y}{4} = \frac{3x - 8}{4} \quad \leftarrow \text{Divide both sides by 4.}$$

$$y = \tfrac{3}{4}x - 2$$

The slope is $\frac{3}{4}$ and the y-intercept is -2.

Because the *y*-intercept is -2, $(0, -2)$ is one of the points on the graph.

Use the slope to find at least one more point on the graph. Start at the point $(0, -2)$, move up 3 units on the *y*-axis (change in *y*), and across 4 units on the *x*-axis (change in *x*). A second point on the graph is $(4, 1)$. Draw a line through the two points $(0, -2)$ and $(4, 1)$.

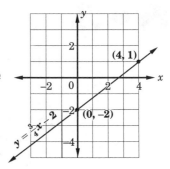

The graph of the line with a slope of $\frac{3}{4}$ and a *y*-intercept of -2 shown at right.

◥ Focus on the Idea

The slope of the graph of $y = mx + b$ is m. The y-intercept is b.

Practice

Find the slope and the *y*-intercept of the graph of each equation. The first one is done for you.

1. $y = -2x - 5$ 2. $2y = 6x - 1$ 3. $2x + 3y = 12$

   slope -2 _____   _____

   y-intercept -5 _____   _____

Write the equation of the line with the given slope and *y*-intercept. The first one is done for you.

4. slope = 2, *y*-intercept = 5 $y = 2x + 5$
5. slope = 4, *y*-intercept = -1 _____
6. slope = $-\frac{5}{2}$, *y*-intercept = 12 _____
7. slope = $\frac{2}{3}$, *y*-intercept = -1 _____

Apply the Idea

8. A wheelchair ramp with a slope of $\frac{1}{8}$ leads from a sidewalk to a doorway 6 inches above the sidewalk. If you think of the sidewalk as the *x*-axis and the doorway as the *y*-axis, what equation can represent the ramp? _____

✎ Write About It

9. Describe the difference between a line with a slope of $\frac{1}{5}$ and a line with a slope of 5.

_____

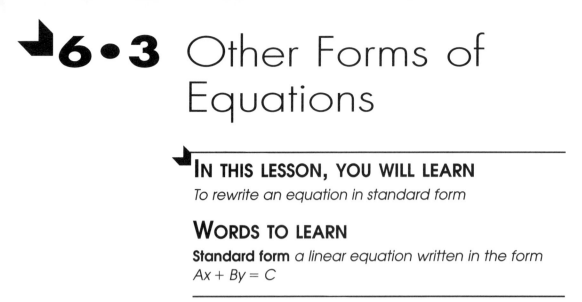

6•3 Other Forms of Equations

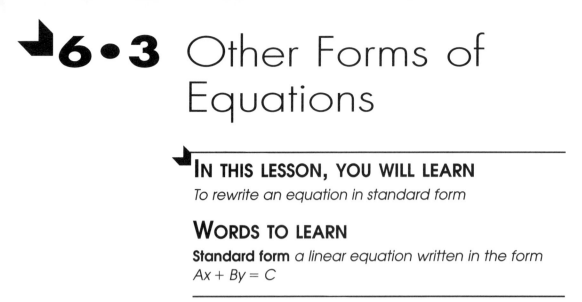

IN THIS LESSON, YOU WILL LEARN

To rewrite an equation in standard form

WORDS TO LEARN

Standard form *a linear equation written in the form*
$Ax + By = C$

The relationship of Unit price × Number of units sold = Income shows how to find income based on sales. If six items are sold at $15 each and four items are sold at $23 each, (6 • $15) + (4 • $23) equals total income. Using variables, if *A* items are sold at $*x* each and *B* items are sold at $*y* each, the total income, *I*, is $Ax + By$, or $Ax + By = I$.

New Idea

A linear equation written in the form $Ax + By = C$ is in **standard form** (STAN-duhrd fawrm). The standard form often shows real-world data more clearly than the slope-intercept form.

Example: Tickets sell for $36 and $24. The total income from ticket sales is $288,000. Write and graph an equation.

Let x = number of $36 tickets.
Let y = number of $24 tickets.

Then, $36x + 24y = 288,000$ (standard form).

Rewrite the equation in slope-intercept form.

$$36x + 24y = 288,000 \qquad \leftarrow \text{Standard form}$$
$$36x - 36x + 24y = -36x + 288,000 \qquad \leftarrow \text{Subtract } 36x \text{ from both sides.}$$
$$\frac{24y}{24} = \frac{-36x + 288,000}{24} \qquad \leftarrow \text{Divide both sides by 24.}$$
$$y = -1.5x + 12,000 \qquad \leftarrow \text{Slope-intercept form}$$

The slope is -1.5. The y-intercept is 12,000. Each point on the line is a solution to the equation, thus a possible combination of $36 and $24 tickets.

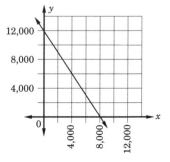

◤ Focus on the Idea

A linear equation written in the form Ax + By = C is in standard form.

Practice

Write each equation in standard form. The first one is done for you.

1. $3y - 8 = 5x + 2$

$-5x + 3y - 8 = 2$

$-5x + 3y = 2 + 8$

$-5x + 3y = 10$

2. $y = 4x - 3$

3. $4x - 7 = 9y$

4. $12 - 6y = 9 + 2x$

5. $0 = 2(2x - 5y + 1)$

6. $y = \frac{4}{5}x - \frac{2}{3}$

Write each equation in slope-intercept form. Then graph it.

7. $x - 2y = -4$

8. $3x + 3y = -9$

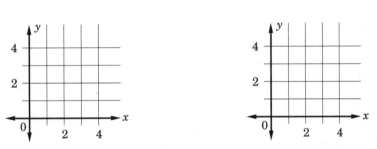

Apply the Idea

9. One Saturday, Eve worked x hours at \$6 per hour and y hours at \$8 per hour. She earned \$48. Write an equation in standard form expressing her earnings.

✏ Write About It

10. To help solve a word problem, sometimes you must first write an equation in standard form. Write such a word problem.

↴6•4 Graphing Absolute-Value Equations

IN THIS LESSON, YOU WILL LEARN

To graph absolute-value equations

WORDS TO LEARN

Absolute-value equation *an equation that involves the absolute value of a variable*

Computer games have come a long way since the first one was invented in the 1970s. The first computer game was a simple one known as Pong. Two players bounced a slowly moving blip back and forth at each other, as in the game of Ping-Pong. A graph of the path that the Pong blip travels looks like the graph of an absolute-value equation.

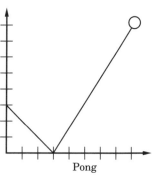
Pong

New Idea

An **absolute-value equation** (AB-suh-loot VAL-yoo ee-KWAY-zhuhn) is any equation involving the absolute value of a variable. When you graph an absolute-value equation, you can allow x to be any number and y will always be positive.

↰Remember

Absolute value is the distance between a number and zero. Absolute value is always a positive number.

Example: Graph this absolute-value equation. $y = |x - 3|$

To draw the graph of the equation $y = |x - 3|$, start by making a table of values. Write several x-values in the table. For each value of x, solve for y. Then plot the points on a coordinate grid. Connect the points.

x	0	1	2	3	4	5
y	3	2	1	0	1	2

You can see that the graph of an absolute-value equation looks like the blip in a game of Pong. It moves in one direction in a straight line, hits the x-axis, then "bounces" back in a different direction in a straight line.

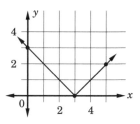

Focus on the Idea

Graph an absolute-value equation by making a table of values. Plot a point for each pair of values. Connect the points.

Practice

Let $y = |x + 2|$. **Find y for each value of x. The first one is done for you.**

1. $x = 6$

$y = |x + 2|$

$y = |6 + 2|$

$y = |8|$

$y = 8$

2. $x = 1$

3. $x = -5$

4. $x = -8$

5. Let $y = |x + 4|$. Complete the table of values by finding a value for y for each value of x.

x	-6	-5	-4	-3	-2
y					

For each equation, make a table of values. Then graph the equation.

6. $y = |x|$

x			
y			

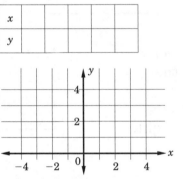

7. $y = |\frac{1}{2}x - 2|$

x				
y				

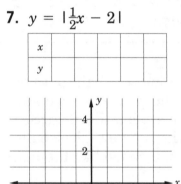

Apply the Idea

8. The graph shows a contractor's design for the roof of a utility shed. The graph of which equation shows the shape of the roof? _____

a. $y = |x| - 6$ **b.** $y = -|6x|$

c. $y = 6 - |x|$

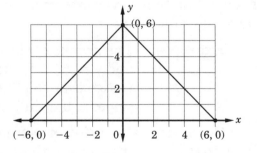

Write About It

9. Is the graph of the equation $y = 2x$ the same as the graph of the equation $y = |2x|$? Explain.

_____

_____

▸6•5 Other Graphs and Their Equations

▸**IN THIS LESSON, YOU WILL LEARN**

To recognize the graphs of parallel lines and perpendicular lines

To recognize the graph of one form of a quadratic equation

WORDS TO LEARN

Parallel lines *lines in the same plane that never intersect, or cross*

Perpendicular lines *lines that intersect to form a right angle*

Quadratic equation *an equation in the form* $y = ax^2 + bx + c$

Parabola *the graph of a quadratic equation of the form* $y = ax^2 + bx + c$

The basic laws concerning the flight path of an unpowered object launched from the ground were discovered by the Italian engineer and mathematician Niccoló Tartaglia (1499–1557). The paths of arrows, baseballs, and rockets can be graphed to form a shape like the figure at the right.

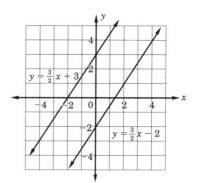

New Idea

Parallel lines (PAR-uh-lehl lynez) are lines in the same plane that never intersect, or cross. Parallel lines have the same slope.

Example: The graphs of the equations $y = \frac{3}{2}x + 3$ and $y = \frac{3}{2}x - 2$ form parallel lines. Notice that the lines have the same slope, $\frac{3}{2}$, but different y-intercepts.

Perpendicular lines (per-puhn-DIHK-yoo-luhr) are lines that intersect to form a right angle. Perpendicular lines have slopes whose product is -1.

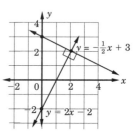

Example: The graphs of the equations $y = 2x - 2$ and $y = -\frac{1}{2}x + 3$ form perpendicular lines. Notice the product of their slopes: $2 \cdot -\frac{1}{2} = -1$.

A **quadratic equation** (kwah-DRAT-ihk ee-KWAY-zuhn) is an equation that has one variable squared. A quadratic equation can be written in the form $y = ax^2 + bx + c$. The graph of a quadratic equation forms a **parabola** (puh-RAB-o-lah), which is a curve like the one drawn by Tartaglia that you saw at the beginning of this lesson.

Focus on the Idea

The slopes of parallel lines are the same. The slopes of perpendicular lines have a product of −1. The graph of a quadratic equation of the form $y = ax^2 + bx + c$ is a parabola.

Practice

Write the equations in slope-intercept form if they are not already in that form. Then state whether each pair of lines is *parallel, perpendicular,* or *neither.* The first one is done for you.

1. $y = 3x + 5$ and $y = -\frac{1}{3}x - 6$ _____perpendicular_____

2. $y = -4x + 1$ and $y = -4x - 5$ _____

3. $y = 2x + 1$ and $x + 2y = 2$ _____

4. $x + y = 4$ and $2x + y = 4$ _____

Find the slope of each line.

5. A line parallel to $3y = 12x - 5$ _____

6. A line perpendicular to $x + 5y = 10$ _____

7. A line parallel to the line through $(2, -5)$ and $(0, 7)$ _____

8. A line perpendicular to the line through $(4, 1)$ and $(-1, -2)$ _____

Apply the Idea

9. A ball tossed into the air follows a path given by the equation $y = -\frac{2}{5}x^2 + 4x$. Complete the table of values for the equation. Then draw the graph.

x	0	2	4	5	6	8	10
y							

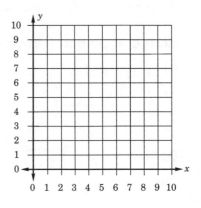

Write About It

10. Suppose you are given the slope of a line. Describe a way of finding the slope of a line perpendicular to it.

_____

_____

Chapter 6 Review

In This Chapter, You Have Learned
- To identify and find rate of change
- To graph a linear equation using the slope and the y-intercept
- To rewrite an equation in standard form or slope-intercept form
- To graph absolute-value equations
- To recognize the graphs of parallel lines, perpendicular lines, and one form of a quadratic equation

Words You Know

From the lists of "Words to Learn," choose the word or phrase that best completes each statement.

1. _____ lines intersect at right angles.
2. A(n) _____ equation contains an x^2 term.
3. The equation $y = 3x + 5$ is written in _____ form.

More Practice

Find the slope of the line that passes through the given points.

4. $(4, 2)$ and $(1, 5)$ _____
5. $(6, -3)$ and $(4, -11)$ _____

Write the equation of the line with the given slope and y-intercept.

6. slope = 3, y-intercept = -2 _____
7. slope = $-\frac{3}{4}$, y-intercept = 4 _____

Find the slope and y-intercept of the graph of each equation.

8. $y = x + 1$ 9. $3y = 12x + 6$

   _____   _____

   _____   _____

10. $10x + 5y = 25$ 11. $7x = 14y - 21$

   _____   _____

   _____   _____

Write each equation in standard form.

12. $3y = 4x - 1$ _____

13. $2(x + 3y - 4) = 0$ _____

Find the slope of each line.

14. A line parallel to $y = -5x + 10$ _____

15. A line perpendicular to $2x - 5y = 4$ _____

Complete a table of values and then graph each equation.

16. $y = |x - 1|$ **17.** $y = x^2 - 6$

x					
y					

x					
y					

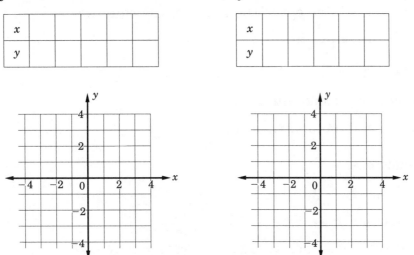

Problems You Can Solve

18. The annual number of labor strikes in the United States fell from 412 in 1969 to 35 in 1992. Find the annual rate of change in the number of strikes. _____

19. The bottom of a painter's ladder stands 5 feet from a wall. The top of the ladder leans against the wall 12 feet above the ground. If the ground is like the x-axis and the wall is like the y-axis, what is the slope of the ladder? _____

20. For Your Portfolio Work with a partner. Find an open area beside a wall. Construct a "launch pad" at a 45° angle at one end of the wall. By flicking a finger, launch a ball of paper at 45° along the wall. Note the shape of the ball's flight path, its highest point, its landing point, and any other details about its flight. Repeat as many times as you think necessary. Then tell what you believe Niccoló Tartaglia, mentioned in Lesson 6•5, discovered about the path of an object launched at a 45° angle.

_____

_____

_____

_____

_____

Chapter 6   Practice Test

1. Find the slope of the line that passes through the points $(-3, 2)$ and $(5, 6)$. _____

2. Find the equation of a line with a slope of -2 and a y-intercept of -6. _____

3. Find the slope and y-intercept of the graph of the equation $12x + 3y = 18$. _____

Use the equation $4x = 5(y - 1)$.

4. Write the equation in slope-intercept form. _____

5. Write the equation in standard form. _____

Find the slope of each line.

6. A line parallel to $-2x + 2y = 5$ _____

7. A line perpendicular to $4x + 6y = -3$ _____

8. Between 1980 and 1986, the average price received by U.S. farmers for 100 pounds of rice fell from \$12.80 to \$3.75. Find the annual rate of change in the price received per 100 pounds. _____

Complete a table of values and then graph each equation.

9. $y = |x + 4|$

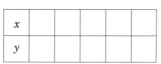

10. $y = -x^2 + 4$

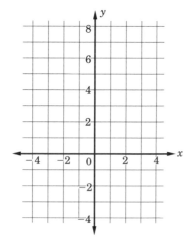

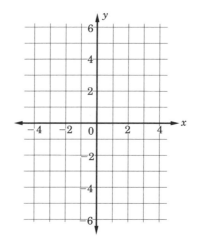

Chapter 7
Exponents

OBJECTIVES:

In this chapter, you will learn

- *To recognize and understand exponents*
- *To use scientific notation to write large and small numbers*
- *To simplify exponential expressions involving multiplication*
- *To simplify exponential expressions involving division*
- *To use negative exponents*
- *To understand the meaning of a zero exponent*
- *To use zero exponents*
- *To understand square roots and cube roots*

Which falls faster, a bowling ball or a marble? Four centuries ago, the Italian astronomer and physicist Galileo Galilei did experiments to find out. According to legend, Galileo dropped a heavy object and a light object at the same time from the top of Italy's Leaning Tower of Pisa. His observations proved that both objects fell at the same rate.

Galileo found that the formula $d = 16t^2$ shows the relationship between the distance an object falls and the time it takes to fall from a height. To find the distance, *d*, that an object falls, multiply 16 by the *square* of the number of seconds, *t*, it has been falling.

Because 2 in the formula $d = 16t^2$ is an exponent, we say that distance increases *exponentially* as an object falls. In this chapter, you will continue the study of exponents that you began in Chapter 1.

↴7•1 More About Exponents

↴IN THIS LESSON, YOU WILL LEARN

To recognize and understand exponents

WORDS TO LEARN

Square *the multiplication of a factor by itself to form a product*

Cube *the multiplication of a factor by itself two times to form a product*

Doubling creates large numbers very quickly. A newspaper page is about $\frac{1}{400}$ inch thick. If you doubled a page by folding it in half, the combined thickness would be $\frac{1}{400} \cdot 2 = \frac{1}{200}$ inch. If you doubled it again, the thickness would be $\frac{1}{100}$ inch. If you could double the page just 25 times, the stack would be more than a mile thick. If you could double it 50 times, the stack would be 44 million miles thick, and would reach nearly halfway to the sun!

↷Remember

You can use a base and an exponent to write the product of a number multiplied by itself.

$$7 \cdot 7 \cdot 7 \cdot 7 = 7^4 \leftarrow \text{Exponent}$$
$$\uparrow$$
$$\text{Base}$$

New Idea

When you **square** (skwair) a number, you multiply it by itself. The product $5 \cdot 5$ can be written 5^2. This is read "5 squared." The word *square* is used because the area of a square with a side measuring s units is s^2.

When you **cube** (kyoob) a number, you use that number three times as a factor. The product $8 \cdot 8 \cdot 8$ can be written 8^3. This is read "8 cubed." The word *cube* is used because the volume of a cube with a side measuring s units is s^3.

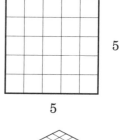

5

5

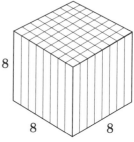

8

8   8

↴Focus on the Idea

A number that is used as a factor two times is squared. A number that is used as a factor three times is cubed.

Practice

Write each product in exponential form. The first one is done for you.

1. $6 \cdot 6 \cdot 6 \cdot 6$ _____6^4_____

2. $4 \cdot 4 \cdot 4 \cdot 4 \cdot 4$ _____

3. $2 \cdot 2 \cdot 2 \cdot 2 \cdot 2 \cdot 2 \cdot 2$ _____

4. $13.7 \cdot 13.7 \cdot 13.7$ _____

Write each expression as a product using a repeating factor.

5. 3^5 _____

6. 20^4 _____

7. 9 squared _____

8. 11 cubed _____

9. x^6 _____

10. n squared _____

Evaluate each expression.

11. 11^1 _____

12. 10^4 _____

13. 5 cubed _____

14. 3^4 _____

15. $(2^3)^2$ _____

16. $(3^2)^3$ _____

17. The value of 2^{20} is 1,048,576. Find the value of 2^{21}. _____

18. The value of p^2 is 64. Find the value of p^3. _____

19. Is the value of 2^3 equal to the value of 3^2? Show your calculations to support your answer.

_____

Apply the Idea

20. A ball or sphere with a radius of r centimeters has a surface area to the nearest hundredth of $12.56r^2$ square centimeters. It has a volume of $4.19r^3$ cubic centimeters. The radius of a basketball is 12 centimeters, or $r = 12$. Find the surface area of the basketball. Then find the volume of the basketball.

_____

Write About It

21. What is the difference between multiplying a number by two and finding the value of the square of a number?

_____

_____

↴7•2 Writing Very Large and Very Small Numbers

↴IN THIS LESSON, YOU WILL LEARN

To use scientific notation to write very large and very small numbers

WORDS TO LEARN

Scientific notation *a number written as the product of a number greater than or equal to 1 and less than 10, and a power of 10*

Money put in an interest-bearing savings account can grow quickly. Any amount saved at 6% interest will double every 12 years. If the Roman emperor Julius Caesar had invested $1 in a 6% savings account 2,000 years ago, his investment today would be worth about $409,000,000,000,000,000,000,000,000,000,000,000,000,000,000!

New Idea

Scientific notation (sy-uhn-TIHF-ihk noh-TAY-shuhn) is a method for writing very large and very small numbers, using exponents. In scientific notation, you write a number as the product of a number greater than or equal to 1 and less than 10, and a power of 10. To write a very large number in scientific notation:

Step 1   Move the decimal point to the left until there is only one digit to the left of the decimal point. Count the number of decimal places the decimal point moved.

Step 2   Drop zeros to the right of the decimal point if they are not needed as placeholders.

Step 3   Write the new number as a factor times 10 to the power of the number you obtained in Step 1.

Example: Write 37,500 in scientific notation.

3.7,500.   ← Move the decimal point 4 places to the left.

3.75   ← This number is greater than 1 and less than 10. Drop the zeros to the right of the decimal point if they are not needed as placeholders.

$3.75 \cdot 10^4$ ← Write the number as a factor times 10 to the fourth power.

To change a very large number from scientific notation to standard form, perform all the steps in the reverse order.

Example: Write $7.3 \cdot 10^6$ in standard form.

$7.300000 \cdot 10^6 \leftarrow$ Add zeros to the right of the decimal point.

$7.300000. \quad \leftarrow$ Move the decimal point 6 places to the right.

$7,300,000 \quad \leftarrow$ Add commas.

✓ Check the Math

1. Vladimir says that the number $45.6 \cdot 10^3$ is in scientific notation. Is he correct? Explain your answer.

_____

◢ Focus on the Idea

A number written in scientific notation is expressed as the product of a number between 1 and 10 and a power of 10.

Practice

Write *yes* or *no* to tell whether or not the number is in scientific notation. The first one is done for you.

2. $6.12 \cdot 10^2$ _____yes_____

3. $21.8 \cdot 10^8$ _____

4. $30.609 \cdot 10^3$ _____

5. $8.09 \cdot 10^1$ _____

6. $5.01 \cdot 10^6$ _____

7. $10.3 \cdot 10^7$ _____

Complete by writing the correct digit for the number of places to move the decimal point. Then write the correct exponent for the power of 10. The first one is done for you.

8. To write 37,800 in scientific notation, move the decimal point __4__ places to the left. The number $37,800 = 3.78 \cdot$ __10^4__.

9. To write 2,900,000 in scientific notation, move the decimal point _____ places to the left. The number $2,900,000 = 2.9 \cdot$ _____.

10. To write 465,200,000 in scientific notation, move the decimal point _____ places to the left. The number $465,200,000 = 4.652 \cdot$ _____.

Write each number in scientific notation.

11. 7,000,000 _____

12. 4,360 _____

13. 53,070 _____

14. 90,310,000 _____

15. 88,008,000,000 _____

16. 50,470,000,000 _____

Write each number in standard form.

17. $9.356 \cdot 10^5$ _____

18. $1.44 \cdot 10^7$ _____

19. $3.07 \cdot 10^3$ _____

20. $6.204 \cdot 10^4$ _____

Extend the Idea

Scientific notation also can be used to write very small numbers, numbers less than 1. To write a very small number in scientific notation, follow these steps.

Step 1   Move the decimal point to the right until there is only one digit to the left of the decimal point.

Step 2   Count the number of decimal places the decimal point moved.

Step 3   Drop any zeros to the left of the first non-zero digit.

Step 4   Write the new number as a factor times 10 to the negative power of the number you obtained in Step 2.

Negative exponents show very small numbers. A fraction such as $\frac{1}{100}$, or $\frac{1}{10^2}$, may be written as 10^{-2}.

Example: Write 0.00062 in scientific notation.

0.0006.2   ← Move the decimal 4 places to the right.

6.2   ← Drop the zeros to the left of the first non-zero digit.

$6.2 \cdot 10^{-4}$ ← Write the number as a factor times 10 to the negative fourth power.

To change a very small number from scientific notation to standard form, perform all the steps in the reverse order.

Example: Write $2.7 \cdot 10^{-6}$ in standard form.

000002.7   ← Add zeros to the left of the first digit.

0.000002.7   ← Move the decimal point 6 places to the left. Add another zero to the left of the decimal point.

21. Which of the following numbers is a very large number, $3.4 \cdot 10^8$ or $4.3 \cdot 10^{-9}$? Explain your answer.

_____

_____

Practice

Write each number in scientific notation.

22. 0.096 _____

23. 0.000932 _____

24. 0.0000705 _____

25. 0.000005810 _____

26. 0.00000047 _____

27. 0.005206 _____

Write each number in standard form.

28. $1.38 \cdot 10^{-5}$ _____

29. $7.064 \cdot 10^{-3}$ _____

30. $8.03 \cdot 10^{-2}$ _____

31. $1.005 \cdot 10^{-6}$ _____

Apply the Idea

32. The dimensions of a machine part must be correct to within 0.005 centimeters. Write 0.005 using scientific notation.
_____

33. The value of a $1 investment after 2,000 years was given at the beginning of the lesson. Write that amount, using scientific notation. _____

34. The earth is $9.3 \cdot 10^7$ miles from the sun. Write this number in standard form. _____

✏ Write About It

35. Many scientists use scientific notation in their work. Think of an area of science that uses very large or very small numbers. Explain how scientific notation might help scientists do their work.

_____

_____

_____

_____

_____

7•3 Multiplication Properties of Exponents

To simplify exponential expressions involving multiplication

WORDS TO LEARN

Exponential expressions *expressions with numbers or variables using exponents*

The world's population was 4 billion in 1975. The United Nations estimates that the world's population is doubling every 35 years. If the growth rate does not change, what do you think the population will be in the year 2010? in 2045? in 2080?

New Idea

Exponential expressions (eks-puh-NEHN-shuhl eks-PREH-shuhnz) are expressions with numbers or variables using exponents. There are three rules that can be used to make these expressions easier to read.

The Product Property of Exponents

To multiply numbers with the same base, you can add the exponents.
$$a^x \cdot a^y = a^{x+y}$$

Example: Simplify. $3^4 \cdot 3^5$

$$3^4 \cdot 3^5 = (3 \cdot 3 \cdot 3 \cdot 3) \cdot (3 \cdot 3 \cdot 3 \cdot 3 \cdot 3)$$

$$= 3^{4+5} \quad \leftarrow \text{Add exponents.}$$

$$= 3^9$$

The Power Property of Exponents

When a number with an exponent is raised to an exponent, you can multiply the exponents.
$$(a^x)^y = a^{xy}$$

Example: Simplify. $(2^6)^4$

$$(2^6)^4 = 2^6 \cdot 2^6 \cdot 2^6 \cdot 2^6$$

$$= 2^{6 \cdot 4} \quad \leftarrow \text{Multiply exponents.}$$

$$= 2^{24}$$

The Power of a Product Property

When a product is raised to an exponent, you can raise each factor to the indicated power.

$$(ab)^x = a^x \cdot b^x$$

Example: Simplify. $(2h)^3$

$$(2h)^3 = (2h)(2h)(2h)$$

$$= 2^3 h^3 \leftarrow \text{Raise each factor to the indicated power.}$$

$$= 8h^3$$

Focus on the Idea

To simplify products containing the same base, you can use the multiplication properties of exponents.

Practice

Simplify each expression. The first two are done for you.

1. $6^2 \cdot 6^5$ _____ 6^7 _____   2. $(6^2)^5$ _____ 6^{10} _____

3. $9^4 \cdot 9^3$ _____   4. $(9^4)^3$ _____

5. $(2^7)^3$ _____   6. $2^7 \cdot 2^3$ _____

7. $(5k)^3$ _____   8. $(3p)^3$ _____

9. $a^4 \cdot a^7$ _____   10. $m^8(m^3)$ _____

11. $(x^2 y^3)^2$ _____   12. $(2^3 n^4)^2$ _____

Apply the Idea

13. The 1920 population of a city doubled, doubled a second time, doubled a third time, then doubled a fourth time by 1990.

    a. If p stands for population, then $p \cdot 2$ stands for the population after it doubled for the first time. Write an exponential expression for the 1990 population.

    _____

    b. How many times greater than the 1920 population is the 1990 population? _____

Write About It

14. Is the value of $5^3 \cdot 5^4$ the same as the value of $(5^3)^4$? Explain your answer.

    _____

    _____

Division Properties of Exponents

▸**In this lesson, you will learn**

To simplify exponential expressions involving division

Words to Learn

Exponential growth *a quantity that grows by a power of the original quantity*

A hospital lab technician grows bacterial cultures. Bacteria usually follow a pattern of **exponential growth** (eks-puh-NEHN-shul grohth). This means they grow according to a pattern that follows a power of the original quantity. The number of bacteria in one kind of culture doubles every hour. At 6 P.M., the culture contained 2^{20} bacteria. How many bacteria had it contained at 4 P.M.?

New Idea

There are two rules that can be used to simplify exponential expressions involving division.

The Quotient Property of Exponents

To divide numbers with the same base, you subtract the exponents.

$$\frac{a^x}{a^y} = a^{x-y}$$

Example: Simplify. $\frac{7^5}{7^2}$

$$\frac{7^5}{7^2} = \frac{\cancel{7} \cdot \cancel{7} \cdot 7 \cdot 7 \cdot 7}{\cancel{7} \cdot \cancel{7}} \quad \leftarrow \text{Cancel out common factors from numerator and denominator.}$$

$$= 7 \cdot 7 \cdot 7$$

$$= 7^3$$

Notice that the expression could have been simplified by subtracting the exponents.

$$\frac{7^5}{7^2} = 7^{5-2}$$

$$= 7^3$$

The Power of a Quotient Property

When a quotient is raised to an exponent, you can raise the numerator and the denominator to that exponent.

$$\left(\frac{a}{b}\right)^x = \left(\frac{a^x}{b^x}\right)$$

Example: Simplify. $\left(\frac{k}{2}\right)^4$ (In this expression, $\frac{k}{2}$ is raised to an exponent.)

$$\left(\frac{k}{2}\right)^4 = \frac{k}{2} \cdot \frac{k}{2} \cdot \frac{k}{2} \cdot \frac{k}{2}$$
$$= \frac{k^4}{2^4}$$
$$= \frac{k^4}{16}$$

Focus on the Idea

To simplify quotients containing the same base, you can use the division properties of exponents.

Practice

Simplify each expression. The first two are done for you.

1. $\frac{3^8}{3^3}$ _____ 3^5 _____

2. $\left(\frac{2}{3}\right)^3$ _____ $\frac{8}{27}$ _____

3. $\frac{5^5}{5^3}$ _____

4. $\frac{9^6}{9^5}$ _____

5. $\frac{10^7}{10^3}$ _____

6. $\frac{4^{11}}{4}$ _____

7. $\left(\frac{1}{2}\right)^5$ _____

8. $\left(\frac{3}{10}\right)^4$ _____

9. $\left(\frac{a}{4}\right)^3$ _____

10. $\left(\frac{m}{n}\right)^9$ _____

11. $\frac{16x^6}{8x^2}$ _____

12. $\frac{45p^{10}}{9p^2}$ _____

Apply the Idea

13. A culture of bacteria in a lab was described on page 118. How many times greater was the number of bacteria at 6 P.M. than at 4 P.M.? _____

14. The diameter of the earth is about $1.28 \cdot 10^7$ meters. The diameter of the sun is about $1.39 \cdot 10^9$ meters. Use the Quotient Property of Exponents to find about how many times bigger the sun's diameter is than the earth's diameter.

_____

Write About It

15. Make up a division problem with large numbers and explain how you can use scientific notation and the rules for exponents to find the answer to your problem.

_____

_____

_____

◀ 7•5 Negative Exponents

WORDS TO LEARN
Nanosecond *one-billionth of a second*

A **nanosecond** (NAN-oh-sek-uhnd) is one-billionth of a second, or $1 \cdot 10^{-9}$ second. Electricity travels a distance of about 1 foot in a nanosecond. This means that, if a light switch is 20 feet from a light, the light will go on about 20 nanoseconds after you flick on the switch.

New Idea

You have learned that, when you write a number less than 1 in scientific notation, you use a negative exponent of 10. Negative exponents can be used with any base other than zero. The meaning of a negative exponent is given by this rule: $a^{-n} = \frac{1}{a^n}$.

Example: Evaluate. 3^{-2}

$$3^{-2} = \frac{1}{3^2}$$
$$= \frac{1}{3 \cdot 3}$$
$$= \frac{1}{9}$$

Simplify. $\frac{x^4}{x^7}$ Then write it, using a positive exponent.

$$\frac{x^4}{x^7} = x^{4-7}$$
$$= x^{-3}$$
$$= \frac{1}{x^3}$$

Simplify. $\frac{12x^{-2}}{4x^5}$ Then write it, using a positive exponent.

$$\frac{12x^{-2}}{4x^5} = \frac{12}{4} \cdot x^{-2-5}$$
$$= 3x^{-7}$$
$$= \frac{3}{x^7}$$

▲ Focus on the Idea
For any nonzero base a, $a^{-n} = \frac{1}{a^n}$.

Practice

Evaluate each expression. The first one is done for you.

1. $2^{-3} = \frac{1}{2^3}$

   $\quad\;\; = \frac{1}{2 \cdot 2 \cdot 2}$

   $\quad\;\; = \frac{1}{8}$

2. 4^{-3}

3. 5^{-2}

4. 3^{-4}

5. 2^{-7}

6. 10^{-5}

7. 1^{-5}

8. 9^{-1}

9. 12^{-2}

Simplify each expression. Then write it, using a positive exponent.

10. $\frac{3^2}{3^5}$ _____

11. $\frac{2^{13}}{2^{21}}$ _____

12. $\frac{n^4}{n^5}$ _____

13. $\frac{k^3}{k^8}$ _____

14. $7y^{-3}$ _____

15. $\frac{b^{-2}}{b^3}$ _____

16. $\frac{10p^6}{2p^{-3}}$ _____

17. $\frac{-18m^{-4}}{9m^{-2}}$ _____

18. $c^{11} \cdot c^{-15}$ _____

19. $(12z^4)^{-1}$ _____

20. $(2k^2)^{-3}$ _____

21. $\frac{21x^2y^{-4}}{7x^{-5}y^{-6}}$ _____

Apply the Idea

22. The formula $P = 5F \cdot \frac{D^{-2}}{4}$ gives the approximate pressure, P, produced by a force, F, acting on a piston of diameter, D. Write the formula using positive exponents. _____

Write About It

23. Tell whether you agree or disagree with this statement: The number 1 raised to any exponent equals 1. Explain your reasoning.

_____

_____

◢7•6 The Exponent of Zero

WORDS TO LEARN

Repeated subtraction *a method for dividing that involves counting how many times one number can be subtracted from another*

The traditional Navajo (NAV-uh-hoh) use a method of division called **repeated subtraction** (ruh-PEE-tehd suhb-TRAK-shuhn). For example, to divide 40 by 8, subtract 8 again and again until you get 0.

$$40 \boxed{-8} = 32, \ 32 \boxed{-8} = 24, \ 24 \boxed{-8} = 16, \ 16 \boxed{-8} = 8, \ 8 \boxed{-8} = 0$$

Because you subtract five 8's to get 0, $40 \div 8 = 5$.

You can use this repeated subtraction method to divide 32 by 32.

$$32 \boxed{-32} = 0 \text{ You subtracted only one 32 to get 0.}$$

Because you subtract one 32 to get 0, $32 \div 32 = 1$.

Now, see how this applies to exponents.

Since $\frac{32}{32} = 1$, and $32 = 2^5$, then $\frac{2^5}{2^5} = 1$.

New Idea

You have worked with positive and negative exponents. The exponent of zero is a special case, because zero is neither positive nor negative. You can use the Quotient Property of Exponents to learn the meaning of a zero exponent.

Example: Evaluate. $\frac{3^7}{3^7}$

According to the Quotient Property:

$\frac{3^7}{3^7} = 3^{7-7} = 3^0$

Also, $\frac{3^7}{3^7} = 1$. If $\frac{3^7}{3^7} = 3^0$ and $\frac{3^7}{3^7} = 1$, then $3^0 = 1$.

You can use the same reasoning to find the value of any number raised to a zero exponent.

Zero Exponent Rule
For any nonzero base b, $b^0 = 1$.

Focus on the Idea

Any nonzero base raised to the exponent zero equals 1.

Practice

Simplify each expression. The first one is done for you.

1. 7^0 _____1_____

2. 3^0 _____

3. 16^0 _____

4. 112.45^0 _____

5. x^0, if $x \neq 0$ _____

6. $(9ab^2)^0$ _____

7. $\frac{5^6}{5^6}$ _____

8. $\frac{m^8}{m^8}$ _____

9. $3k^0$ _____

10. $-15p^0$ _____

11. $4ab^0$ _____

12. $\frac{15c^0}{3c^4}$ _____

13. $\frac{24h^5k^3}{3hk^0}$ _____

14. $32n^4(5v^2)^0$ _____

15. Complete the table. The first one is done for you.

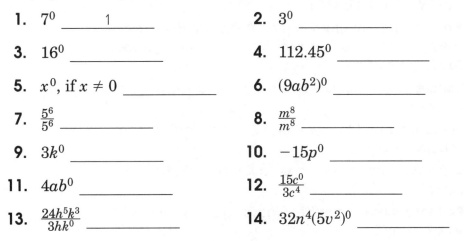

2^4	2^3	2^2	2^1	2^0	2^{-1}	2^{-2}	2^{-3}	2^{-4}
16								

16. Solve for n. $x^7(x^n) = 1$ _____
17. Solve for y. $(3y)^8 = 1$ _____

Apply the Idea

18. Suppose you invest P dollars in a savings account at i percent interest compounded annually. The amount A in the account after n years is given by $A = P(1 + i)^n$. For what value of n will the amount in the account equal the amount you originally invested? _____

Write About It

19. Tell whether you agree or disagree with this statement: Two raised to any exponent equals a positive number. Explain your reasoning.

_____

_____

↴7•7 Radicals

To understand square roots and cube roots

WORDS TO LEARN

Pythagorean Theorem *in a right triangle, the square of the hypotenuse is equal to the sum of the squares of the lengths of the two legs*

Square root *a number whose square equals a given number*

Radical symbol *the symbol √, which indicates a square root*

Cube root *a number whose cube equals a given number*

Perfect square *a number whose square root is a whole number*

The Greek mathematician Pythagoras (6th Century B.C.) is best remembered for his study of right triangles. The **Pythagorean Theorem** (py-thag-uh-REE-uhn THEE-uh-ruhm) states that, in a right triangle, the sum of the squares of the lengths of the two legs equals the square of the length of the hypotenuse. This means that in right triangle ABC, we can write
$$a^2 + b^2 = c^2.$$

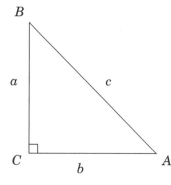

New Idea

Finding the **square root** (skwair root) of a number is the inverse, or opposite, of squaring the number. If a is the square root of a number n, then $a \cdot a$ or a^2 equals n.

The **radical** (RAD-ih-kuhl) **symbol**, $\sqrt{}$, indicates a square root. If a number is written inside the symbol, you find the square root of that number.

Example: Find the square root of 9, or $\sqrt{9}$.

Squaring	*Square root*
$3^2 = 9$	$\sqrt{9} = 3$

Read "3 squared is 9" and "the square root of 9 is 3."

Since $3^2 = 9$ and $(-3)^2 = 9$, both 3 and -3 are square roots of 9.

Use $\sqrt{}$ to indicate a positive value and $-\sqrt{}$ to indicate a negative value.

Finding the **cube root** (kyoob root) of a number is the inverse of cubing the number. If a is the cube root of a number n, then

$$a \cdot a \cdot a = a^3$$
$$a^3 = n$$
$$a = \sqrt[3]{n}$$

The symbol $\sqrt[3]{}$ indicates a cube root.

Example: Find the cube root of 64, or $\sqrt[3]{64}$.

<table>
<tr><td>Cubing</td><td>Taking the cube root</td></tr>
<tr><td>$4^3 = 64$</td><td>$\sqrt[3]{64} = 4$</td></tr>
</table>

Read "4 cubed is 64" and "the cube root of 64 is 4."

Since $(-4)^3 = -64$, the number 64 has only one cube root, which is 4.

✓ **Check the Math**

1. Marisa wrote $\sqrt[3]{x^6} = x^2$. Is she correct? Explain your answer.

_____

◤ **Focus on the Idea**

A square root is a number whose square is a given number. A cube root is a number whose cube is a given number.

Practice

Simplify. Then check. The first two are done for you.

2. $\sqrt{49} = 7$

    Check: $7 \cdot 7 = 49$

3. $\sqrt{25x^6} = 5x^3$

    Check: $5x^3 \cdot 5x^3 = 25x^6$

4. $\sqrt{81}$

5. $-\sqrt{16}$

6. $-\sqrt{1}$

7. $\sqrt{100}$

8. $\sqrt[3]{8}$

9. $\sqrt[3]{1}$

10. $\sqrt{64h^2}$

11. $-\sqrt{\dfrac{49}{100}}$

Write *true* or *false*.

12. $\sqrt{16} \cdot \sqrt{9} = 4 \cdot 3$ _____   **13.** $\sqrt{16} + \sqrt{9} = 4 + 3$ _____

Extend the Idea

A **perfect square** is a number whose square root is a whole number. The numbers 1, 4, 9, 16, and 25 are perfect squares because:

$$\sqrt{1} = 1 \qquad \sqrt{4} = 2 \qquad \sqrt{9} = 3 \qquad \sqrt{16} = 4 \qquad \sqrt{25} = 5$$

Suppose you want to find the square root of a number that is *not* a perfect square. Here are two ways to approximate this kind of square root.

Example: Find the approximate square root of 46, $\sqrt{46}$, using perfect squares.

Write an inequality using one perfect square that is less than 46 and one that is greater than 46.

$\sqrt{36} < \sqrt{46} < \sqrt{49}$ ←Find the square root
$\quad 6 < \sqrt{46} < 7 \qquad$ of each perfect square.

Now you know that $\sqrt{46}$ is between 6 and 7.

The number 6.5 is halfway between 6 and 7.

Compare $\sqrt{46}$ and 6.5.

Square 6.5. $(6.5)^2 = 42.25$, so $\sqrt{42.25} = 6.5$.

You know $46 > 42.25$, so $\sqrt{46} > \sqrt{42.25}$. That means $\sqrt{46} > 6.5$.

The whole number 7 can be used to estimate the $\sqrt{46}$.

Find the approximate square root of 46, $\sqrt{46}$, using a calculator.

Find the $\sqrt{}$ key on your calculator.

Some calculators use two keys for finding square roots:

INV $\boxed{x^2}$ or **2nd** $\boxed{x^2}$

Press $\boxed{4}\boxed{6}\boxed{\sqrt{}}$ The display shows that the square root of 46 is 6.7823299.

Rounding the square root to the nearest hundredth, $\sqrt{46} \approx 6.78$.

14. Find $(6.78)^2$. If the answer is not 46, explain why.

_____

🖩 Practice

Find each square root to the nearest tenth.

15. $\sqrt{10}$ _____   **16.** $\sqrt{61}$ _____

17. $\sqrt{2}$ _____   **18.** $\sqrt{23}$ _____

19. $\sqrt{85}$ _____   **20.** $\sqrt{7}$ _____

Find each square root to the nearest hundredth.

21. $\sqrt{18}$ _____   **22.** $\sqrt{40}$ _____

Apply the Idea

Use the Pythagorean Theorem, $a^2 + b^2 = c^2$, to solve exercises 23 to 25.

23. Find the length of the hypotenuse of a right triangle with legs measuring 6 inches and 8 inches. _____

24. A 17-foot ladder is on level ground, leaning against a vertical wall. The top of the ladder is 15 feet above the ground. How far is the bottom of the ladder from the base of the wall?

_____

25. A baseball diamond is really a square measuring 90 feet on a side. Find the distance from home plate to second base. Express your answer to the nearest hundredth. _____

26. A square parking lot has an area of 24,000 square feet. Find the length of one side to the nearest hundredth.

_____

27. The formula $t^2 = \frac{d}{16}$ gives the time t in seconds that it takes an object dropped to fall d feet. (Assume no wind or downward velocity.) A rivet falls from the wing of an airplane flying at an altitude of 36,000 feet. How long, to the nearest tenth, does the rivet take to reach the ground? _____

✎ Write About It

28. Try finding $\sqrt{-16}$ with your calculator. Explain what happens.

_____

_____

Lesson 7•7 *Radicals*   **127**

Chapter 7   Review

In This Chapter, You Have Learned
- To recognize and understand exponents
- To use scientific notation to write large and small numbers
- To simplify expressions containing exponents
- To simplify exponential expressions involving division
- To use negative exponents
- To use zero exponents
- To understand square roots and cube roots

Words You Know

From the lists of "Words To Learn," choose the word or phrase that best completes each statement.

1. The _____ of a number is the product of the number and itself.

2. A(n) _____ is a number whose square root is a whole number.

3. The $\sqrt{}$ symbol is called a(n) _____ .

4. The number of times that a base is used in a product is the _____ .

More Practice

Use a base and an exponent to write each product.

5. $9 \cdot 9 \cdot 9 \cdot 9$ _____   6. $b \cdot b \cdot b$ _____

Evaluate each expression.

7. 2^5 _____   8. 10^5 _____

Write each number, using scientific notation.

9. 64,500 _____   10. 0.0009 _____

11. 0.000000331 _____   12. 100,000,000,000 _____

Write each number, using standard notation.

13. $5 \cdot 10^{-2}$ _____   14. $9.99 \cdot 10^2$ _____

15. $1.0302 \cdot 10^{-6}$ _____   16. $8.11 \cdot 10^7$ _____

Simplify. Write answers with positive exponents.

17. $7^3 \cdot 7^5$ _____

18. $k^4(k^6)$ _____

19. $(3n)^3$ _____

20. $(2^4p)^2(2^3p^4)^4$ _____

21. 2^{-3} _____

22. $6^4 \cdot 6^{-8}$ _____

23. $\frac{5^9}{5^{10}}$ _____

24. $(\frac{c}{7})^4$ _____

25. $\frac{12x^3}{6x^{-3}}$ _____

26. $9h^5(3h^{-5})$ _____

Simplify.

27. $\sqrt{81}$ _____

28. $\sqrt{\frac{9}{64}}$ _____

29. $-\sqrt{49x^8}$ _____

30. $\sqrt{\frac{16}{25}}$ _____

Problems You Can Solve

31. The formula $T = 6.28\sqrt{\frac{L}{32}}$ gives the length of time T, in seconds, that it takes a pendulum of length L, in feet, to complete one swing. Find T for a pendulum 1 foot in length, to the nearest tenth. _____

32. The formula $v = \sqrt{2.5r}$ gives the maximum velocity, in miles per hour, at which a car can go around a curve of radius r feet without skidding. Find the maximum velocity for a curve of radius 1,000 feet. _____

33. For Your Portfolio In 1992, U.S. car makers produced $5.6 \cdot 10^6$ automobiles. In September, 1993, the Congressional Budget Office estimated that the savings and loan crisis would cost the U.S. government $1.8 \cdot 10^{11}$ dollars.

The news each day is full of big numbers. Cut out examples, like the ones above, of how five very large or very small numbers are used in newspapers or magazines. Write the numbers, using both scientific and standard notation, and explain what each number represents.

_____

_____

_____

_____

_____

_____

Chapter 7   Practice Test

Use a base and an exponent to write each product.

1. $3 \cdot 3 \cdot 3 \cdot 3 \cdot 3 \cdot 3$ _____   2. $x \cdot x \cdot x \cdot x$ _____

Evaluate each expression.

3. 5^3 _____   4. $2^5 \cdot 2^3$ _____

5. n^0 _____   6. 6^{-2} _____

Write each number, using scientific notation.

7. 0.00067 _____   8. $456,000,000$ _____

Write each number, using standard notation.

9. $2 \cdot 10^3$ _____   10. $8.001 \cdot 10^{-5}$ _____

Simplify. Express your answers with positive exponents.

11. $8^4 \cdot 8^5$ 12. $n^3(n^7)$ 13. $(3a)^4$

_____   _____   _____

14. $5^{-2}(5^{-3})$ 15. $\dfrac{x^4}{x^6}$ 16. $\left(\dfrac{c}{2}\right)^5$

_____   _____   _____

17. $\dfrac{24y^5}{8y^8}$ 18. $\sqrt{x^8}$ 19. $\sqrt[3]{8}$

_____   _____   _____

20. The formula $v = \sqrt{20m}$ can be used to find the velocity in miles per hour, v, of a car that leaves a skid mark m feet in length after the driver slams on the brakes. If the car leaves a skid mark 200 feet long, find the velocity of the car to the nearest tenth.

_____

Chapter 8

Inequalities

OBJECTIVES:

In this chapter, you will learn

- *To graph an inequality*
- *To recognize the difference between the graph of an equality and the graph of an inequality*
- *To solve inequalities in one step*
- *To solve inequalities in two steps*

In much of your study of mathematics, you have looked for exact answers. But mathematics is not always about finding exact answers. Sometimes a *range*, or span, of answers is needed. For example, instead of $x = 5$, the solution to a problem might be $x > 5$. This means that x can be any number greater than 5. An expression like $x > 5$ is called an inequality.

Inequality symbols
$<$ means "less than"
$\leq$ means "less than or equal to"
$>$ means "greater than"
$\geq$ means "greater than or equal to"

Inequalities are often found in the rules for sports. A rule for football states that the ball must weigh from 14 to 15 ounces. Letting w = the weight of a football, the rule can be written $w \geq 14$ and $w \leq 15$.

For the weight of a football, any weight (w) in the entire range of numbers from 14 ounces to 15 ounces is satisfactory.

8•1 Equations and Inequalities

In addition to a salary, a salesperson is often paid a commission, which is a certain percent of total sales. The percent is called the commission rate. Sometimes the commission rate increases as total sales increase. For example, the commission rate may increase when total sales are greater than $20,000. We could write this using symbols as $s > 20,000$.

New Idea

An inequality is a mathematical sentence that states that two expressions are not equal. An inequality can have more than one solution. The following **inequality symbols** (ihn-ee-KWAK-uh-tee SIHM-buhlz) show the relationships between numbers.

$<$ means "less than" $\qquad$ $\leq$ means "less than or equal to"

$>$ means "greater than" $\qquad$ $\geq$ means "greater than or equal to"

The solution to an equation can be graphed on a number line. A solid black dot at 2 represents the solution to the equation $x = 2$.

The solution to an inequality can also be graphed on a number line. Look at the graphs below. An arrow continues in either direction (left or right) indefinitely. All the numbers in that direction are included in the solution. These numbers make up the solution set.

$x < 2$ $\qquad$ $x \leq -3$ $\qquad$ $x > -1$ $\qquad$ $x \geq 1$

The number at the endpoint of each arrow is *included* (closed dot) in an inequality with $\leq$ or $\geq$. The number at the endpoint is *not included* (open dot) in an inequality with $<$ or $>$.

Example: Solve the inequality $x + 3 < 5$.

Think about possible values of x. The values $\{-3, -2, -1, 0, 1\}$ make the inequality true. The values $\{2, 3, 4, 5, 6\}$ make the inequality false. Look back at the graph of the first inequality on page 132. It shows the solution to the inequality $x + 3 < 5$, which is $x < 2$.

◤ **Focus on the Idea**

To graph an inequality, draw an arrow to indicate the direction of the solution. Draw an open or closed dot to indicate whether or not the endpoint is included.

Practice

Write the inequality that is graphed on the number line. The first one is done for you.

1.
$$\text{1 2 3 4 5}$$
$x < 4$

2.
$$-7\ -6\ -5\ -4\ -3\ -2$$
_____

3.
$$-3\ -2\ -1\ 0\ 1$$
_____

4.
$$1\ 2\ 3\ 4\ 5$$
_____

Label the number line. Then graph each inequality.

5. $x \geq -1$

6. $x < -3$

7. $x \leq 4$

8. $x > 0$

Write the solution set for each inequality.

9. $x + 2 < 7$ _____

10. $x - 3 > 1$ _____

11. $x + 6 \leq 9$ _____

12. $2x \geq 8$ _____

Apply the Idea

13. Geoff is a computer salesperson. His commission is 5% of the first $20,000 and 8% of the additional sales. If his sales totaled $65,000, find his earnings for the month. _____

Write About It

14. An elevator sign reads, "No more than 10 persons allowed." Explain the meaning of "no more than 10" in algebraic terms.

_____

8•2 Solving One-Step Inequalities

IN THIS LESSON, YOU WILL LEARN

To solve inequalities in one step

WORDS TO LEARN

Tolerance range of error a measurement can have and still be correct

The **tolerance** (TAHL-uhr-uhns) of a measurement is the range of error that is permitted. For example, a tool designer may give the width of a machine part as 3.57 ± 0.01 centimeters. (Read $\pm$ as *plus or minus*.) If w stands for width, then $3.57 - 0.01 \le w \le 3.57 + 0.01$.

What is a width that is within the given range of error?

New Idea

You can solve inequalities using the same methods you used to solve equations. You can add or subtract the same number to or from both sides of an inequality just as you can add or subtract the same number to or from both sides of an equation. You can multiply or divide both sides of an inequality by the same positive number. In each case, the direction of the inequality symbol remains the same.

Examples:

$$x + 8 \le 20$$
$$x + 8 - 8 \le 20 - 8$$
$$x \le 12$$

$$\frac{x}{5} < -4$$
$$5 \cdot \frac{x}{5} < 5 \cdot (-4)$$
$$x < -20$$

However, notice what happens when you multiply or divide both sides of an inequality by a *negative* number:

$$-4 < 2 \qquad \leftarrow -4 \text{ is to the left of 2 on a number line.}$$
$$(-5)(-4) > (-5)(2) \qquad \leftarrow \text{Multiply both sides by } -5.$$
$$20 > -10 \qquad \leftarrow \text{Inequality symbol has been reversed.}$$

If you multiply or divide both sides of an inequality by a negative number, you must *reverse* the direction of the inequality symbol to make the inequality true.

Example:

$$-6x > 18 \qquad \leftarrow \text{Divide both sides of the inequality by } -6.$$
$$\frac{-6x}{-6} < \frac{18}{-6} \qquad \leftarrow \text{Reverse the direction of the symbol.}$$
$$x < -3$$

Focus on the Idea

Inequalities can be solved much like equations. When both sides of an inequality are multiplied or divided by a negative number, the direction of the inequality symbol is reversed in the solution.

Practice

State whether the inequality symbol *stays the same* or *should be reversed* in the solution of that inequality. The first one is done for you.

1. $-\frac{1}{5}x > -1$ <u>should be reversed</u>

2. $0 < 10 + y$ _____

3. $x + 18 \geq 58$ _____

4. $-12y \leq 48$ _____

Solve the inequality. The first one is done for you.

5. $-5x > 30$

$\frac{^-5x}{^-5} < \frac{30}{^-5}$

$X < -6$

6. $x - 24 \geq 10$

7. $x + 7 < 2$

8. $-9x \leq -45$

9. $16 < \frac{n}{3.25}$

10. $-x \leq 6$

Apply the Idea

11. The tolerance of the length of a machine part is given as $l \pm 0.03$ centimeters.

   a. Write an inequality for the length showing the given tolerance. _____

   b. If the smallest acceptable length is 10.67 centimeters, find the greatest acceptable length. _____

12. A car mechanic guarantees that the charge, c, for repairing a carburetor, will be between \$30 and \$250. Write two inequalities giving the least and greatest possible charges.

   _____

Write About It

13. Write a word problem to represent $20x < 100$.

   _____

   _____

   _____

8•3 Solving Two-Step Inequalities

IN THIS LESSON, YOU WILL LEARN

To solve inequalities in two steps

WORDS TO LEARN

Budget *a listing of fixed expenses that must be paid out of monthly income*

When writing a budget, a rule of thumb is that three times the amount of rent you pay plus your monthly expenses, or money you owe, should be less than your income. A **budget** (BUJ-iht) is a listing of fixed expenses that must be paid out of monthly income. One way to calculate how much money can be spent on rent is to use an inequality.

If Johann earns $1,600 a month and has monthly expenses of $550, how much can he spend for rent?

New Idea

You have learned how to solve an inequality that involves one step. You identify the operation and apply the inverse operation.

When an inequality contains two steps, solve by applying two inverse operations. First, undo addition or subtraction. Second, undo multiplication or division.

⤳*Remember*

If you multiply or divide both sides of an inequality by a negative number, you must reverse the direction of the inequality symbol.

Example: Solve. $-3x + 2 > 14$

$$-3x + 2 > 14$$
$$-3x + 2 - 2 > 14 - 2 \leftarrow \text{Subtract 2 from both sides}$$
$$-3x > 12 \qquad \text{of the inequality.}$$
$$\frac{-3x}{-3} < \frac{12}{-3} \qquad \leftarrow \text{Divide both sides by } -3 \text{ and}$$
$$x < -4 \qquad \text{reverse the inequality symbol.}$$

Focus on the Idea

To solve a two-step inequality, first undo addition or subtraction. Then undo multiplication or division.

Practice

State the first step you would perform to solve each inequality. The first one is done for you.

1. $3k + 4 > 7$

    subtract 4

2. $\frac{x}{4} - 6 \le 10$

    _____

3. $\frac{x}{-3} + 5 \ge -7$

    _____

Solve each inequality.

4. $\frac{x}{2} + 3 < 7$

    _____

5. $6x - 3 \ge 21$

    _____

6. $-5x - 6 > 14$

    _____

7. $\frac{x}{-6} + 8 \le -5$

    _____

8. $x > 2x - 2$

    _____

9. $\frac{x}{4} > 5 + 7$

    _____

10. $-3x - 8x > 29 - 7$

    _____

11. $19 + 4x \le 7x - 2$

    _____

12. $2(x - 7) \ge 7x + 6$

    _____

Apply the Idea

13. The Redwood Corporation budgeted $1,600 of their monthly expenses for a computer data service. The service costs $300 a month plus $40 per hour of use.

    a. Let h = the number of hours the company uses the service. Write an inequality relating the number of hours of use and the budgeted amount. _____

    b. What is the greatest number of hours the company can use the service each month? _____

14. Refer to the beginning of this lesson on page 136. Write and solve an inequality to determine how much Johann can spend for rent. Show all your work. Then graph the solution on the number line below.

Write About It

15. Work backwards. Write a two-step inequality that has $x \le -10$ as its solution.

    _____

    _____

    _____

In This Chapter, You Have Learned

- To graph an inequality
- To recognize the difference between the graph of an equality and the graph of an inequality
- To solve inequalities in one step
- To solve inequalities in two steps

Words You Know

From the lists of "Words to Learn," choose the word or phrase that best completes each statement.

1. A mathematical statement that two expressions are not equal is a(n) _____.

2. _____ is the range of error a measurement can have and still be correct.

3. A list of expenses that must be paid out of monthly income is a(n) _____.

More Practice

Write the inequality that is graphed on the number line.

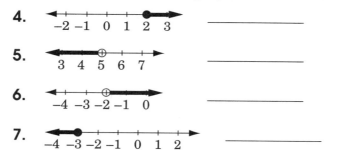

4. _____

5. _____

6. _____

7. _____

Label the number line. Then graph the inequality.

8. $x > 4$ ⟵——————→

9. $x \le 0$ ⟵——————→

10. $x < -3$ ⟵——————→

11. $x \ge -5$ ⟵——————→

State whether the inequality symbol *stays the same* or *should be reversed* in the solution of the given inequality.

12. $x + 8 \le 5$ _____

13. $\frac{x}{6} > 9$ _____

14. $-3x > 45$ _____

15. $\frac{y}{-10} \le 7.5$ _____

State the first step you would perform to solve each inequality.

16. $5x > 15$

_____

17. $3 > \frac{x}{-6}$

_____

18. $5x - 6 \leq 13$

_____

19. $\frac{x}{9} + 14 > 12$

_____

Solve each inequality.

20. $6x > 24$

_____

21. $p - 7 \leq 10$

_____

22. $-2k < 40$

_____

23. $\frac{x}{5} \geq -3$

_____

24. $14 > c + 8$

_____

25. $9 \leq \frac{x}{-3}$

_____

26. $2x - 9 > 11$

_____

27. $6p > 5p + 3$

_____

28. $\frac{h}{4} - 17 \leq -5$

_____

Problems You Can Solve

29. Highlighter markers sell for $3.50 apiece for the first 50, $3.25 apiece for the next 50, and $3.00 apiece for each additional 50.

    a. Write three inequalities, one to describe the number of markers in each price category. Let n represent the number of markers purchased.

    _____

    b. Find the cost of 140 markers. _____

30. **For Your Portfolio** The statement below is taken from a magazine advertisement. If a = the age of Vacation Sweepstakes entrants, then $a \geq 18$.

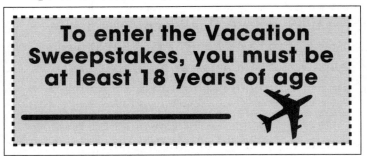

Find two statements in magazines, newspapers, or books that can be written as inequalities. Look for terms like "at least," "no less than," "between," and "at most." On a sheet of paper, write each statement exactly as you find it, or tape it onto the paper. Then write and graph an inequality that represents the statement.

Write the inequality that is graphed on the number line.

1.
−4 −3 −2 −1 0 1 2

_____

2.
−3 −2 −1 0 1 2

_____

Label the number line. Then graph the inequality.

3. $x \leq 3$

4. $x > -2$

State whether the inequality symbol *stays the same* or *should be reversed* in the solution of the given inequality.

5. $-8x < 4$

_____

6. $5x + 8 > 53$

_____

7. $3(x + 7) \leq -45$

_____

8. $4.8x \geq 48$

_____

9. $x + 5 < -10$

_____

Solve each inequality.

10. $4x \geq 20$

_____

11. $x - 9 < 5$

_____

12. $-6k < 30$

_____

13. $12 \leq p + 7$

_____

14. $\frac{n}{-7} < -5$

_____

15. $-3.5 > -x$

_____

16. $5n + 2 < 3n - 8$

_____

17. $3(8 - x) \leq 5(2x - 3)$

_____

18. $x - \frac{3}{2}x < 7 - 11$

_____

Solve.

19. Elaine earns a monthly salary of $800 plus a commission of 4% on her total sales. She wants to make at least $3,000 per month. Let s = total sales. Write and solve an inequality to find the total sales Elaine must make each month.

_____

20. A worker wants to assemble an average of nine or more lamps per hour during a 7-hour shift. In the first hour, the worker assembled three lamps. Let n = the number of lamps the worker must assemble each remaining hour. Write and solve an inequality. _____

Monomials and Polynomials

◀**OBJECTIVES:**

In this chapter, you will learn

- *To identify a polynomial that is a monomial, binomial, or trinomial*
- *To identify the degree of a polynomial*
- *To add polynomials*
- *To subtract polynomials*
- *To find the simplest form of a polynomial, using addition and subtraction*
- *To multiply a polynomial by a monomial*
- *To multiply two binomials*
- *To multiply two polynomials*

You have used variables and expressions throughout your study of algebra. Some of these expressions are polynomials, which are used in formulas from geometry and science. Some of these formulas follow.

$V = s^3$	volume of a cube
$V = lwh$	volume of a rectangular prism
$V = \pi r^2 h$	volume of a cylinder
$V = \frac{4}{3}\pi r^3$	volume of a sphere
$S = 6s^2$	surface area of a cube
$S = 2(lw + lh + wh)$	surface area of a rectangular prism
$S = 2\pi r^2 + 2\pi rh$	surface area of a cylinder
$S = 4\pi r^2$	surface area of a sphere
$C = \frac{5}{9}(F - 32)$	convert temperature from degrees Fahrenheit to degrees Celsius
$d = rt$	distance formula, given rate and time
$d = \frac{1}{2}gt^2$	distance traveled by a freely falling object

9•1 Recognizing Monomials and Polynomials

IN THIS LESSON, YOU WILL LEARN

To identify a polynomial that is a monomial, binomial, or trinomial

To identify the degree of a polynomial

WORDS TO LEARN

Polynomial *an algebraic expression made up of one or more terms*

Monomial *a term that is a number, a variable, or the product of a number and one or more variables*

Binomial *a polynomial with two terms*

Trinomial *a polynomial with three terms*

Degree of a term *the sum of the exponents of the variables in a term*

Degree of a polynomial *the greatest of the degrees of the terms of a polynomial*

A *polygon* is a geometric shape with many sides. You know that a *monorail* has one track, a *bicycle* has two wheels, and a *tricycle* has three wheels. Based on this, what do you think an algebraic expression with two terms is called? An algebraic expression with three terms? An expression with five terms?

Remember

Like terms are terms whose variable parts are the same. An expression is in simplest form when no more operations can be performed and it has no like terms.

New Idea

Any algebraic expression that contains one or more terms is called a **polynomial** (pahl-ih-NOH-mee-uhl). An expression with one term is called a **monomial** (mah-NOH-mee-uhl), with two terms is called a **binomial** (by-NOH-mee-uhl), and with three terms is called a **trinomial** (try-NOH-mee-uhl).

The **degree of a term** (dih-GREE) is the sum of the exponents of all the variables. The degree of the term $2x^3$ is 3. The degree of the term $5a^2bc^3$ is $2 + 1 + 3$, or 6. The **degree of the polynomial** is the greatest of the degrees of the terms of a polynomial. The degree of the polynomial $2x^3 + 5x^2 + 4x + 7$ is 3.

Focus on the Idea

You can describe a polynomial by its number of terms. The degree of a polynomial is the greatest of the degrees of the terms.

Practice

Tell whether each expression is a monomial, a binomial, or a trinomial. The first one is done for you.

1. $4 + 2x - 3x^2$ ___trinomial___
2. $3z$ _____

3. $4x + \frac{3}{4}$ _____
4. $29x^2 + 17$ _____

State the degree of the term. The first one is done for you.

5. $5a^3b$ ___4___
6. a^2b^2c _____

7. $\frac{1}{2}m^3$ _____
8. $2x$ _____

State the degree of the polynomial. The first one is done for you.

9. $6t^2 + 8t^4$ ___4___
10. $5t^4 - 3t^2$ _____

11. $x + x^2 + x^3 + x^4 + x^5$ ___
12. $12x + 36x^3$ _____

Name the like terms. The first one is done for you.

13. $3b, 3b^2, 7b, b^3, 4b$ ___3b, 7b, 4b___

14. $x, 3x, 2x^2, 9x, x^3$ _____

15. $2ac^2, 2a^2c, 8ac, 9ac^2, 2a^2c^2$ _____

Apply the Idea

16. The volume of a cube is found by the formula $V = s^3$, where s is the length of an edge. Write the volume for each of these three cubes.

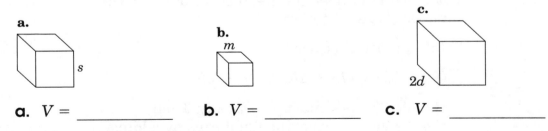

a. $V =$ _____
b. $V =$ _____
c. $V =$ _____

Write About It

17. The formula for the volume of a prism, $V = lwh$, contains a monomial with degree 3. Explain why this is true.

_____

_____

9•2 Adding and Subtracting Polynomials

IN THIS LESSON, YOU WILL LEARN

To add polynomials

To subtract polynomials

To find the simplest form of a polynomial, using addition and subtraction

WORDS TO LEARN

Simplify a polynomial *to combine the like terms of a polynomial*

Jason works in the shipping department of a shoe manufacturer. He has three shipments to prepare. The first shipment calls for eight size-10 boxes and three size-$10\frac{1}{2}$ boxes. The second shipment calls for seven size-10 and two size-$10\frac{1}{2}$ boxes. The third shipment calls for four size-10 and six size-$10\frac{1}{2}$ boxes. How many boxes of each size will Jason need for the three shipments?

New Idea

Add two or more polynomials by adding, or combining, the like terms. Subtract two polynomials by adding the first polynomial to the opposite of each like term in the second polynomial. **Simplify a polynomial** (SIHM-pluh-fy, pahl-ih-NOH-mee-uhl) by combining all the like terms in the polynomial.

Examples: Find how many boxes of each size Jason needs.

Let a = the number of size-10 boxes and b = the number of size-$10\frac{1}{2}$ boxes.

Total number of boxes:

$(8a + 3b) + (7a + 2b) + (4a + 6b)$

$$
\begin{array}{r}
8a + 3b \\
7a + 2b \\
\underline{4a + 6b} \\
19a + 11b
\end{array}
$$
← Line up vertically. Then combine like terms by adding.

Jason needs 19 size-10 boxes and 11 size-$10\frac{1}{2}$ boxes to complete these shipments.

Subtract. $(9x^3 + 2x^2 + 5x + 6) - (3x^3 + x)$

$$
\begin{array}{l}
9x^3 + 2x^2 + 5x + 6 \\
\underline{-(3x^3 \qquad\quad + x \quad)}
\end{array}
\rightarrow
\begin{array}{l}
9x^3 + 2x^2 + 5x + 6 \\
\underline{+(-3x^3 \qquad\quad - x \quad)} \\
6x^3 + 2x^2 + 4x + 6
\end{array}
$$

Focus on the Idea

To add two or more polynomials, you simplify or combine like terms. To subtract polynomials, you add the terms in the first polynomial to the opposite of each like term in the second polynomial.

Practice

Add or subtract, then simplify. The first two are done for you.

1. $(3n + 7) + (2n - 6)$
   $(3n + 2n) + (7 - 6)$
   $5n + 1$

2. $(4a^2 + a + 4) - (a^2 + 5)$
   $$
   \begin{array}{l}
   (4a^2 + a + 4) \\
   \underline{-(a^2 \qquad + 5)} \\
   3a^2 + a - 1
   \end{array}
   $$

3. $3ab + 19ab$

4. $(x + 3) - (x + 9)$

5. $(2x^2 + 7) - (2x - 9)$

6. $(2x^2 - 7) + (12x^2 + 3x + 3)$

7. $(3x^2 + 2x - 9) - (4x^2 - 4x)$

8. $(x + 3) + (2x - 7) + (3x + 4)$

Apply the Idea

9. Jason has the three large boxes shown here ready to go to the Walker Shoe Store. The trucking company wants to know the total volume of the boxes. Jason knows he can find the volume of each box by multiplying its length times its width times its height. What expression should Jason give for the total volume?

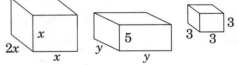

✏ Write About It

10. You know that when you add or subtract measurements, only like terms can be added or subtracted. Write an example of a situation for which you might need to add or subtract measurements. How is this like adding or subtracting polynomials? How is it different?

_____

_____

Multiplying a Polynomial by a Monomial

IN THIS LESSON, YOU WILL LEARN
To multiply a polynomial by a monomial

WORDS TO LEARN
Term *the parts of a variable expression separated by addition or subtraction signs*

The manager of the Book City Warehouse needs to divide the warehouse into sections for different kinds of books. Each section has width w and length $w + 15$. Find an expression that shows the area of one of the sections.

New Idea

You can use the Distributive Property of Multiplication Over Addition to multiply a polynomial by a monomial. Multiply each **term** in the polynomial by the monomial. (See Lesson 2•1.) Then simplify by combining like terms.

Examples: Write an expression for the area of a section of the warehouse.

The area of a section of the warehouse is found by multiplying $(w + 15)$ by w.

Area $(A) = w(w + 15)$

$A = (w \cdot w) + (w \cdot 15)$ ← Multiply each term by w.

$A = w^2 + 15w$ ← Simplify.

Write an expression for the entire area of the warehouse.

Multiply the area of one section by 4.

$A = 4(w^2 + 15w)$

$A = (4 \cdot w^2) + (4 \cdot 15w)$ ← Multiply each term by 4.

$A = 4w^2 + 60w$ ← Simplify.

✓ **Check Your Understanding**

Simplify each product.

1. $9(3rw)$ _____

2. $3a(4a + 5ab)$ _____

Focus on the Idea

To multiply a polynomial by a monomial, multiply each term of the polynomial by the monomial. Simplify each term and combine like terms.

Practice

Simplify each product. The first one is done for you.

3. $2x^2(7x)$

$2 \cdot x^2 \cdot 7 \cdot x$

$(2 \cdot 7) \cdot (x^2 \cdot x)$

$14 \cdot x^3$

4. $5n(3n + 8)$

5. $4ab(6a + 5b)$

6. $3(2x^2 + 3x + 6)$

7. $8x(5x^2 - 5x - 8)$

8. $n(n^5 + n^4 + n^3 + n^2 + n)$

Multiply. The first one is done for you.

9. $a + 8$ by $7a^2$

$7a^2(a + 8)$

$(7a^2 \cdot a) + (7a^2 \cdot 8)$

$7a^3 + 56a^2$

10. $x^2 + 7x$ by $2x$

11. $2x^2 + 3x - 6$ by $4x$

12. $3v^3 - 2v^2 - 7v - 9$ by $-7v$

13. $-9(st^2 + st - 9)$

14. $6acd(a^2 + 3ac - 4d)$

15. $-6(-2k^2 + 2k - 6)$

16. $2m^3(2m^3 - 10m + 7)$

Extend the Idea

To multiply a polynomial by a monomial with several variables, first write the products. Then simplify, using the Associative and Commutative Properties.

Example: Multiply. $13ab(4a + 6b)$

$$13ab(4a + 6b)$$

$$(13 \cdot 4 \cdot a \cdot a \cdot b) + (13 \cdot 6 \cdot a \cdot b \cdot b)$$

$$52a^2b + 78ab^2$$

✓Check the Math

17. Jacob multiplied $5x^2 + 7x + 2$ by $6x^3$. He wrote $30x^5 + 42x^4 + 12x^3 = 84x^{12}$. What did he do wrong?

_____

Practice

Simplify. The first one is done for you.

18. $-x^3(2x^2 + 2x + 5)$

$(-x^3 \cdot 2x^2) + (-x^3 \cdot 2x) + (-x^3 \cdot 5)$

$-2x^5 - 2x^4 - 5x^3$

19. $5abc(2a^2 + 3b^2 + 4c^2)$

20. $2a^2b^3c^4(2a - 2b - c)$ **21.** $-2x^2y^2z^2(xyz + xy + yx)$

22. $8rst(8r^3st^2 + 3rs^2t + 4rst + 8)$

Apply the Idea

23. Refer to the diagram of Book City Warehouse at the beginning of this lesson. Book City Warehouse rents floor space at a rate of $92 per square foot. What expression represents the cost of renting one of the four sections?

_____

24. The Alonzo Distribution Center wants to rent a section in the warehouse. They found that w is equal to 38 feet. What will be the cost of renting the section? Write the equation and solve it.

_____

_____

_____

Write About It

25. Look at your answers for exercises 18 to 22. Explain how you used the Associative, Commutative, and Distributive Properties to find your answers. Give an example of the use of each property from one of the exercises.

_____

_____

_____

_____

9•4 Multiplying Polynomials

IN THIS LESSON, YOU WILL LEARN

To multiply two binomials
To multiply two polynomials

WORDS TO LEARN

FOIL method *a procedure used for multiplying two binomials*

Martina is framing a rectangular picture. The mat that surrounds the picture is $1\frac{1}{2}$ inches wider than the picture on the left and right sides. It is 2 inches longer than the picture at the top and bottom. Martina wants to cover both the picture and mat with a piece of glass. She needs to find the total area of the picture and mat.

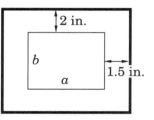

New Idea

The product of two polynomials can be found, using the Distributive property. Multiply each term in the first factor by each term in the second factor.

Example: What is the total area of the picture and mat?

To find the total area, Martina needs to know the picture's length and its width. The width of the mat is $1\frac{1}{2} + 1\frac{1}{2}$ or 3 inches more than the width of the picture. The length is $2 + 2$ or 4 inches more than the length of the picture.

Let the binomial $(a + 3)$ stand for the total width of the mat. Let the binomial $(b + 4)$ stand for the total length. Find the area of the glass by multiplying $(a + 3)(b + 4)$.

Use the Distributive Property. Multiply each term in the first factor by the second factor.

$(a + 3)(b + 4)$

$a(b + 4) + 3(b + 4)$

$(a \cdot b) + (a \cdot 4) + (3 \cdot b) + (3 \cdot 4)$ ← Use the
                                                                                         Distributive
$ab + 4a + 3b + 12$ Property again.

The area of the picture and mat can be expressed by $ab + 4a + 3b + 12$.

The Distributive Property also can be applied to multiplying a binomial and a trinomial.

Example: Multiply. $(x + 3)(x^2 - 2x - 5)$

$$(x + 3)(x^2 - 2x - 5)$$

$$x(x^2 - 2x - 5) + 3(x^2 - 2x - 5)$$

$$(x \cdot x^2 + x \cdot -2x + x \cdot -5) +$$
$$(3 \cdot x^2 + 3 \cdot -2x + 3 \cdot -5)$$

$$x^3 + -2x^2 + -5x + 3x^2 + -6x + -15$$

$$x^3 + x^2 - 11x - 15$$

✓ Check Your Understanding

Find the product.

1. $(n - 2)(n^2 + n + 3)$ _____

▶ Focus on the Idea

To multiply two polynomials, you can use the Distributive Property by multiplying each term of the first factor by each term in the second factor.

Practice

Multiply. The first one is done for you.

2. $(n + 2)(n + 3)$
   n(n + 3) + 2(n + 3)
   n² + 3n + 2n + 6
   n² + 5n + 6

3. $(n - 4)(n + 5)$

4. $(n + 5)(n^2 + 2n + 7)$

5. $(2x - 3)(5x + 8)$

6. $(x - 2)(x^2 + 3x + 6)$

7. $(2n - 1)(n^2 - 6n + 8)$

8. $(x + 3)(y - 5)$ **9.** $(3x + 2)(x^2 - 5x - 12)$

10. $(3n + 5)(2n^3 + 3n^2 + 5n - 4)$ **11.** $(x^2 + 3x - 7)(2x^2 - x + 4)$

Extend the Idea

The **FOIL method** (eff-oh-eye-ehl meh-thud) is a procedure used to multiply two binomials. The letters F, O, I, and L, indicate the pairs of terms that have to be multiplied.

Example: Use FOIL to multiply $(x + 3)(x + 5)$.

    F   The first terms are multiplied. $(x + 3)(x + 5)$ $x \cdot x$, or x^2

    O   The outer terms are multiplied. $(x + 3)(x + 5)$ $x \cdot 5$, or $5x$

    I   The inner terms are multiplied. $(x + 3)(x + 5)$ $x \cdot 3$, or $3x$

    L   The last terms are multiplied. $(x + 3)(x + 5)$ $3 \cdot 5$, or 15

$x^2 + 5x + 3x + 15$ ← Add the terms and simplify, if necessary.

$(x + 3)(x + 5) = x^2 + 8x + 15$

✓Check the Math

12. Tanner multiplied $(x + 3)$ and $(x - 2)$ using the FOIL method. He wrote:

     First terms: $x \cdot x$, or x^2
     Outer terms: $x \cdot -2$, or $-2x$
     Inner terms: $3 \cdot x$, or $3x$
     Last terms: $3 \cdot -2$, or -6

     $(x + 3)(x - 2)$ $= x^2 - 2x + 3x - 6$

Is Tanner correct? Has he simplified the polynomial? Explain.

_____

_____

Practice

Multiply these binomials. Use the FOIL method. The first one is done for you.

13. $(x + 9)(x + 7)$

$x \cdot x + x \cdot 7 + 9 \cdot x + 9 \cdot 7$

$x^2 + 7x + 9x + 63$

$x^2 + 16x + 63$

14. $(x - 5)(x - 6)$

15. $(x + 2)(x - 9)$

16. $(x - 7)(x + 8)$

17. $(2x + 3)(x + 2)$

18. $(3x - 7)(2x - 3)$

19. $(4x + 7)(7x - 9)$

20. $(2x - 9)(3x + 5)$

Apply the Idea

21. Martina has another picture; its length is 3 times longer than its width. The mat surrounding the picture is 2 inches wide on all four sides. Find the area of a piece of glass that covers the picture and mat.

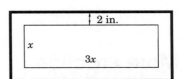

_____

Write About It

22. Explain why the FOIL method only works for multiplying two binomials.

_____

_____

_____

_____

Chapter 9 Review

In This Chapter, You Have Learned
- To identify a monomial, binomial, or trinomial
- To identify the degree of a polynomial
- To add and subtract polynomials
- To find the simplest form of a polynomial
- To multiply two polynomials

Words You Know

Choose the letter of the phrase in column 2 that defines the word or phrase in column 1.

Column 1	Column 2
1. polynomial _____	**a.** a polynomial with three terms
2. degree of a polynomial _____	**b.** a polynomial with two terms
3. FOIL method _____	**c.** an algebraic expression made up of one or more terms
4. trinomial _____	**d.** procedure for multiplying two binomials
5. binomial _____	**e.** the greatest of the degrees of the terms of a polynomial

More Practice

Identify the polynomial as a *monomial, binomial,* or *trinomial.* Then state the degree of the polynomial.

6. $25x^3 + 2x + 3$ _____

7. $4x^6y^3$ _____

8. $3k + 7$ _____

9. $4x^2 + 5x + 17$ _____

Simplify each expression.

10. $(8j + 7) + (3j - 9)$

11. $(5x^2 - 6) + (-2x^2 - 3)$

12. $(12w + 16) - (5w + 8)$

13. $(x^3 + x^2 + 3x) + (2x^2 + 9x)$

14. $(2a^2 + 8ac) - (5ac)$

15. $(7d - 5) - (9d - 7)$

16. $8(4bc)$

_____

17. $4n(n^2 + 3n - 7)$

_____

18. $2ab^2c(3a + 4ab + 5c)$

_____

19. $(x + 4)(x + 8)$

_____

20. $(3x + 4)(2x - 7)$

_____

21. $(2x + 3)(2x^3 + 3x^2 - 4x - 5)$

_____

Problems You Can Solve

22. Tina wants to cover her kitchen cupboards with shelf paper. Each shelf is 18 inches deep. Each cupboard is 36 inches wide and has two shelves. There are six cupboards. A roll of shelf paper covers 1,000 square inches. How many rolls must Tina buy to cover the top of all her shelves? _____

23. Sheelah's hobby is photography. She cuts her own mats before framing her photos. She wants to use mats that add 2 inches to the top, bottom, and both sides of each photo. How much total material will she need for the three mats shown below?

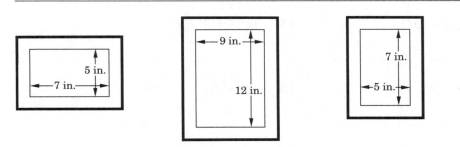

24. Tomás works in a shipping supply store after school. He has to keep the store stocked with the plastic foam "peanuts" used for packing. The peanuts are kept in three large boxes shaped like cubes. He estimates that each peanut measures 1 cubic inch. What is the total volume of the three boxes? About how many peanuts are stored in them?

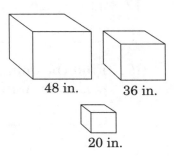

25. For Your Portfolio Formulas are used in mathematics, science, and business. On another sheet of paper, make a list of formulas that use polynomials. Try to find as many formulas as possible that are not listed at the beginning of the chapter. Ask people you know if they use any formulas in their jobs. Some possible uses for formulas might involve finding sales tax, interest, depreciation, flow rates, or machinery ratios.

Chapter 9   Practice Test

Tell whether each polynomial is a *monomial*, *binomial*, or *trinomial*. Then state the degree of the polynomial.

1. $7m + 12$ _____

2. $5x^2y^7$ _____

3. $5x^3 + 12x^2 + 3$ _____

4. $6x^2 + 15x - 3$ _____

Simplify each expression.

5. $(h + 9) + (3h - 8)$

6. $(x^2 - 8) + (2x^2 - 15)$

7. $(6x^2 + 3x + 7x) + (-3x^3 + 7x)$

8. $(x^3 + 4x^2 - 3x) + (5x^2 - 4x)$

9. $(a + 5) - (3a + 8)$

10. $(5k^2 + 8k) - (5k^2 + 11k)$

11. $(9n^2 - 7n) - (6n^2 + n)$

12. $x^3(7x^2y^2)$

13. $9(2x^2 + 9x + 9)$

14. $3x(2x^2 + 6x - 7)$

15. $(b + 6)(b + 8)$

16. $(6x - 7)(2x - 5)$

17. $(x - 3)(2x^3 + 3x^2 + 4x + 5)$

18. $(3x + 4)(x^3 - 2x^2 - 8x - 12)$

19. Find the volume of this rectangular prism. Simplify your answer.

_____

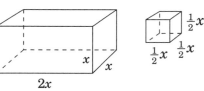

20. Anna put the small box into the large box. Then she added enough plastic foam "peanuts" to the large box to fill it up. Write the expression that represents the volume of foam peanuts Anna added to the large box. Simplify the expression.

_____

Chapter 10

Factoring

OBJECTIVES:

In this chapter, you will learn

- To find the greatest common factor
- To find the greatest common monomial factor
- To factor quadratic expressions
- To factor a difference of two squares
- To factor a perfect square trinomial
- To recognize that if a product of two or more factors is 0, at least one factor must be 0
- To solve quadratic equations that can be factored
- To use the quadratic formula to solve quadratic equations

Do you know what the string of letters and symbols at the right means?

s_lopez@notarealco.com

If you are familiar with computers, you probably know that s_lopez@notarealco.com is an e-mail address. The term *e-mail* refers to computer messages that are sent over telephone lines.

The information before the @ symbol in an e-mail address tells who the message is for or whom it is from. The letters between the @ symbol and the dot give the location of a computer. The last part tells whether a computer is located at a school (edu), at a business (com), or at some other kind of organization.

An e-mail address looks complicated until you know how to break it down into simpler parts. The same is true for some expressions in algebra. In this chapter, you will learn how to rewrite an expression, such as $5k^2 - 19k + 12$, as a product of simpler expressions.

To find the greatest common factor of two or more integers

To find the greatest common factor of two or more monomials

WORDS TO LEARN

Greatest common factor (GCF) *the greatest number or expression that evenly divides two or more numbers or expressions*

Ron bought two sections of railing from an historic baseball stadium. The sections are 48 inches long and 54 inches long. Ron plans to cut both sections into pieces to sell as souvenirs. He wants each piece to be as long as possible. He also wants all of the pieces to be equal in length. How long should Ron make each piece?

New Idea

The **greatest common factor** (GRAYT-uhst KAHM-uhn FAK-tuhr) **(GCF)** is the greatest number, or expression, that is a factor of two or more numbers or expressions. You can find the greatest common factor of two numbers by listing all of the factors of each number.

Examples: Is 2, 3, or −8 a factor of 16?

To determine whether a number is a factor, divide the product by one factor. If the number divides the product evenly, then it is a factor.

$16 \div 2 = 8$ So, 2 is a factor of 16.

$16 \div 3 = 5 \text{ R}1$ So, 3 is not a factor of 16.

$16 \div -8 = -2$ So, −8 is a factor of 16.

By dividing, you can see that 2 and −8 are factors of 16, but 3 is not a factor of 16.

How long should Ron make each piece of railing? Ron made a list of all the possibilities by making a chart of the factors of 48 and 54.

48-inch railing		54-inch railing	
Length (inches)	Number of Pieces	Length (inches)	Number of Pieces
48	1	54	1
24	2	27	2
16	3	18	3
12	4	9	6
8	6	6	9
6	8	3	18
4	12	2	27
3	16	1	54
2	24		
1	48		

Since Ron wants each piece to be the same length, he noticed that both railings could be cut into pieces 1 inch, 2 inches, 3 inches, or 6 inches long. Since Ron wants the pieces to be as long as possible, he should make each piece of railing 6 inches long.

The common factors of 48 and 54 are 1, 2, 3, and 6. Since 6 is the greatest of these, it is the greatest common factor (GCF) of 48 and 54.

✓Check Your Understanding

1. Is 7 a factor of 84? Tell how you know.

_____

◤Focus on the Idea

The greatest number that is a factor of two or more numbers is the greatest common factor (GCF) of the numbers. You can list the factors of each number to help you find the GCF of two integers.

Practice

Write the GCF of each group of integers by listing the factors of each number. The first one is done for you.

2. 20, 25
   20: 1, 2, 4, 5, 10, 20
   25: 1, 5, 25
   The GCF is 5.

3. 45, 65

_____

4. 15, 24

_____

5. 80, 104

_____

6. 12, 30, 42

_____

7. 18, 36, 72

_____

8. 13, 18

_____

9. 8, 15, 49

_____

Extend the Idea

You know that a monomial can be a number, a variable, or a product of a number and one or more variables. You can find the greatest common factor of two monomials by listing all of the factors of each monomial.

Example: Find the GCF of $12x^3y^5$ and $42x^5yz$.

To list all the factors of $12x^3y^5$, list the factors of 12, x^3, and y^5:

12: 1, 2, 3, 4, ⑥, 12 x^3: 1, x, x^2, ⓧ³ y^5: 1, ⓨ, y^2, y^3, y^4, y^5

To list all the factors of $42x^5yz$, list the factors of 42, x^5, y, and z:

42: 1, 2, 3, ⑥, 7, 14, 21, 42 x^5: 1, x, x^2, ⓧ³, x^4, x^5

y: 1, ⓨ   z: 1, z

Find the greatest common factor for the coefficients and each variable: 6, x^3, y

The GCF of $12x^3y^5$ and $42x^5yz$ is $6x^3y$.

✓Check the Math

10.   Isabel found the GCF of $5u^2v^3$ and $20uv^2$ to be $5uv^2$. Did she factor the monomials correctly? How do you know?

_____

Practice

Find the GCF of each group of monomials. The first one is done for you.

11. $6b^3$, $12b$

_6b_ _____

12. $10a$, $15b$

_____

13. $2x^3y$, $8xy^2$

_____

14. $11m^3n^4$, $26m^2n^5$

_____

15. $8r^2s$, $24rst$

_____

16. $27x^2y^2$, $18xy^2$, $21x$

_____

17. $12t^2v$, $25t^2v^2$

_____

18. $30c^7d^4f^6$, $18c^5d^4f^5$, $12c^6d^4f^4$

_____

19. $4g^2h$, $11t^5v^4$, $13xy^3$

_____

20. $30p^9q^6r^8$, $10p^5q^6r^9$, $20pqr$

_____

Apply the Idea

21. Find three monomials whose GCF is $6a^3b^2$.

_____

22. Fernando wants to put some fencing around his rectangular garden. The garden is 24 feet by 40 feet. Fernando wants to use as few fence posts as possible. The posts have to be equally spaced. What is the least number of posts Fernando can use? _____

23. Jeff needs to reduce the fraction $\frac{75}{90}$ to lowest terms. Jeff's teacher said that he could only divide once. By what factor should Jeff reduce the fraction? _____

24. Suppose that, in the example on page 158, Ron bought a third piece of railing that was 64 inches long. Can Ron still cut the equal-sized pieces to be 6 inches? If not, what size pieces should he make? _____

✏ Write About It

25. For the monomials x^2 and x^3, the GCF is x^2. For the monomials x^{23} and x^{25}, the GCF is x^{23}. Will the GCF always be the base raised to the lesser exponent? Explain.

_____

_____

26. Consuela said that since the monomials $12x^3y$ and $7wz^2$ do not have any common factors, there is no GCF. Is she correct? Explain.

_____

_____

10•2 Factoring Expressions

IN THIS LESSON, YOU WILL LEARN

To find the greatest common monomial factor of a polynomial

WORDS TO LEARN

Greatest common monomial factor *the greatest monomial expression that evenly divides all terms of a polynomial*

A teacher wrote the polynomial $18a^3 + 12a^2 - 6a$ on the chalkboard, and asked the students what they knew about it. One student said that it was a third-degree polynomial. Another said that it was a trinomial. The teacher suggested to the students that they think about something "common." Jenny thought for a minute, then raised her hand, and said, "The three terms might have common factors!" The teacher then asked Jenny to name the greatest common factor.

New Idea

When you factor a polynomial, you write it as a product of its factors. The Distributive Property of Multiplication over Addition tells you that $5x(x + 8) = 5x^2 + 40x$. You can also use this property to factor $5x^2 + 40x = 5x(x + 8)$. Factoring a polynomial means finding the greatest common monomial factor of all the individual terms. The **greatest common monomial factor** (GRAYHT-uhst KAHM-uhn moh-NOH-mee-uhl FAK-tuhr) of a polynomial is the greatest expression that divides all terms of a polynomial evenly.

Examples: Help Jenny find the greatest common factor of the polynomial $18a^3 + 12a^2 - 6a$.

List the factors of each term:

$18a^3$: 1, 2, 3, ⑥, 9, 18, ⓐ, a^2, a^3

$12a^2$: 1, 2, 3, 4, ⑥, 12, ⓐ, a^2

$-6a$: $-6, -3, -2, -1, 1, 2, 3,$ ⑥, ⓐ

The GCF of $18a^3 + 12a^2 - 6a$ is $6a$.

To factor the polynomial $18a^3 + 12a^2 - 6a$, divide each term by $6a$ for one factor. The other factor is $6a$.

$$18a^3 + 12a^2 - 6a = 6a(3a^2) + 6a(2a) + 6a(-1)$$

$$= 6a(3a^2 + 2a - 1)$$

1. How could you check your work to see if you have factored correctly?

_____

_____

◤**Focus on the Idea**

Some polynomials can be factored as the product of the greatest common monomial factor and another polynomial, by using the distributive property.

Practice

Find the GCF of each polynomial. The first one is done for you.

2. $4a + 12b$

_____ 4 _____

3. $5p^3 + 10p^2$

_____

4. $16u - 8v + 4$

_____

5. $27x^2 + 7x^2y - 18y$

_____

6. $12s^3 - 6s^2 + 18s$

_____

7. $3x^2y - 9xy - 6x$

_____

Factor each polynomial by finding the GCF. The first one is done for you.

8. $8x^2y - 10xy$

_____ 2xy(4x − 5) _____

9. $14a^4b^2 + 16ab^3$

_____

10. $t^3 + 10t^2 + 5t$

_____

11. $9c^5d^6 + 12c^3d^7$

_____

12. $21z^4 + 24z^3 - 7z$

_____

13. $4m^2n^2 - 6mn$

_____

Extend the Idea

Another way to factor a polynomial is by writing it as a product of two polynomials. One way to factor a trinomial is to reverse the FOIL method you used to multiply two binomials.

$$(x + 4)(x + 5) = (x)(x) + (5)(x) + (4)(x) + (4)(5)$$

First Outer Inner Last

L
I
F
O

$$= x^2 + 5x + 4x + 20$$
$$= x^2 + 9x + 20$$

Example: Use the FOIL method to factor $m^2 + 6m + 8$.

Think of $m^2 + 6m + 8$ as the product of two binomials.

$$m^2 + 6m + 8 = (\quad)(\quad)$$

The FOIL method says that the product of the first terms is m^2. So each first term is m.

$$m^2 + 6m + 8 = (m \quad)(m \quad)$$

The FOIL method says that the product of the last terms is 8. Try 4 and 2 as the last terms.

$$m^2 + 6m + 8 = (m + 4)(m + 2)$$

Multiply your factors to check.

$$(m + 4)(m + 2) = m^2 + 2m + 4m + 8$$
$$= m^2 + 6m + 8$$

The factors are correct.

$$m^2 + 6m + 8 = (m + 4)(m + 2)$$

Suppose you had tried 8 and 1 as last terms instead of 4 and 2. Your binomial product would have been
$$(m + 8)(m + 1) = m^2 + m + 8m + 8$$
$$= m^2 + 9m + 8.$$

This product is not equal to $m^2 + 6m + 8$. So, the factors 8 and 1 are not correct. Some people call this method of factoring a trial-and-error method, because you try different factors and eliminate the ones that do not work. For some polynomials, there are no two factors that are correct; then the expression is not factorable.

✓Check the Math

14. Elsa has factored the expression $x^2 + x - 56$ as $(x - 8)(x + 7)$. Has she factored correctly?

___

Practice

Factor each polynomial by writing it as a product of two binomials. The first one is done for you.

15. $p^2 - 8p + 15$

$\underline{\qquad (p-5)(p-3) \qquad}$

16. $x^2 + 10x + 21$

$\underline{\qquad\qquad\qquad\qquad}$

17. $w^2 - w - 30$

$\underline{\qquad\qquad\qquad\qquad}$

18. $y^2 + 5y + 6$

$\underline{\qquad\qquad\qquad\qquad}$

19. $x^2 - 7x + 12$

$\underline{\qquad\qquad\qquad\qquad}$

20. $m^2 - 7m - 8$

$\underline{\qquad\qquad\qquad\qquad}$

Apply the Idea

21. Ahmed decided that his original garden, shown by the small rectangle at the right, is too small. He decided to increase the size of the garden to the area shown by the large rectangle. Write an expression for the area of Ahmed's new, larger garden. (Remember, area = length • width.)

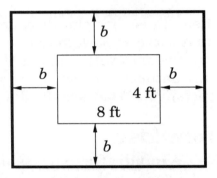

$\underline{\qquad\qquad\qquad\qquad\qquad\qquad\qquad\qquad\qquad}$

Write About It

22. The binomial factors of polynomials in the forms $x^2 - bx - c$ and $x^2 + bx - c$ have one positive sign and one negative sign. How do you decide which factor will have a positive sign and which factor will have a negative sign?

$\underline{\qquad\qquad\qquad\qquad\qquad\qquad\qquad\qquad\qquad}$

$\underline{\qquad\qquad\qquad\qquad\qquad\qquad\qquad\qquad\qquad}$

23. Give at least two ways in which the Distributive Property of Multiplication over Addition can be useful when factoring a polynomial.

$\underline{\qquad\qquad\qquad\qquad\qquad\qquad\qquad\qquad\qquad}$

$\underline{\qquad\qquad\qquad\qquad\qquad\qquad\qquad\qquad\qquad}$

$\underline{\qquad\qquad\qquad\qquad\qquad\qquad\qquad\qquad\qquad}$

Rebecca is a graphic designer. She uses rectangles to create patterns that serve as background for advertisements. Her favorite rectangles are the ones with an area of $2x^2 + 7x + 6$ square inches, where x is any natural number. If x is 4, what are the dimensions of the rectangle? What are the dimensions if x is 6?

New Idea

A **quadratic expression** (kwah-DRAT-ihk eks-PREHSH-uhn) is a polynomial of the form $ax^2 + bx + c$, where a is not equal to zero. You factored polynomials where a was equal to 1. Now you can factor some quadratic expressions where a is not equal to 1 by using the FOIL method.

Examples: What are the dimensions of Rebecca's rectangles?

Because area = length • width, Rebecca will need to find the two factors of $2x^2 + 7x + 6$. Because the product of the first terms of the polynomial factors is $2x^2$, the first terms must be $2x$ and x.

$$2x^2 + 7x + 6 = (2x \qquad)(x \qquad)$$

Since the product of the last terms is 6, the last two factors are either 6 and 1 or 2 and 3. Each pair gives you two possibilities. Keep trying until you get the correct product.

$$(2x + 6)(x + 1) = 2x^2 + 8x + 6$$

$$(2x + 1)(x + 6) = 2x^2 + 13x + 6$$

$$(2x + 2)(x + 3) = 2x^2 + 8x + 6$$

$$(2x + 3)(x + 2) = 2x^2 + 7x + 6$$

The dimensions of the rectangle are $(2x + 3)$ and $(x + 2)$. If x is 4, the dimensions are 11 in. by 6 in. If x is 6, the dimensions are 15 in. by 8 in.

Factor $4x^2 + 4x - 24$.

To factor this polynomial, first notice that each of the terms has a greatest common factor of 4. Start by applying the distributive property.

$$4x^2 + 4x - 24 = 4(x^2 + x - 6)$$

Then factor the trinomial, as in the last lesson.

$$4(x^2 + x - 6) = 4(x + 3)(x - 2)$$

So, $4x^2 + 4x - 24 = 4(x + 3)(x - 2)$.

✓**Check the Math**

1. Pete factored $4x^2 + 4x - 24$ to be $(2x + 6)(2x - 4)$. Can he do any more factoring? Why or why not?

   _____

Practice

Factor each polynomial. The first one is done for you.

2. $3x^2 + 9x + 6$
   $3(x^2 + 3x + 2) = 3(x + 1)(x + 2)$

3. $7a^2 + 15a + 2$

   _____

4. $5w^2 + 4w - 1$

   _____

5. $2x^2 - 11x + 9$

   _____

6. $3n^2 - 9n - 12$

   _____

7. $2a^2 - a - 6$

   _____

8. $10n^2 - 34n + 12$

   _____

9. $11a^2 - 51a - 20$

   _____

10. $4p^2 - 44p + 72$

    _____

11. $5q^2 + 35q + 50$

    _____

Extend the Idea

To factor some quadratic expressions, you will have to try two or more possibilities for the first terms of the factors.

Example: Factor $9n^2 - 6n - 8$.

The product of the first terms is $9n^2$. You could try either $9n$ and n or $3n$ and $3n$ for the first terms. The product of the last terms is -8. The possibilities are $(1)(-8)$, $(-1)(8)$, $(2)(-4)$, and $(-2)(4)$. Keep trying these possibilities until you get the ones that give you the correct product.

$$(9n + 1)(n - 8) = 9n^2 - 71n - 8$$

$$(9n - 1)(n + 8) = 9n^2 + 71n - 8$$

$$(9n + 2)(n - 4) = 9n^2 - 34n - 8$$

$$(9n - 2)(n + 4) = 9n^2 + 34n - 8$$

$$(3n + 1)(3n - 8) = 9n^2 - 21n - 8$$

$$(3n - 1)(3n + 8) = 9n^2 + 21n - 8$$

$$(3n + 2)(3n - 4) = 9n^2 - 6n - 8$$

Notice that the first and last terms are the same for all possible combinations; only the middle term changes.

✓Check Your Understanding

12. Sean wants to factor the expression $4y^2 + 8y + 3$. What are the possible first terms? _____

Practice

Factor each polynomial. The first one is done for you.

13. $6p^2 + 12p + 6$
    $\underline{6(p^2 + 2p + 1) = 6(p + 1)(p + 1)}$

14. $10s^2 + 8s - 2$

    _____

15. $8x^2 + 8x - 16$

    _____

16. $12a^2 + 3a - 42$

    _____

17. $6w^2 + 5w - 4$

    _____

18. $6g^2 - 31g + 5$

_____

19. $8k^2 - 10k + 2$

_____

20. $4a^2 + 32a - 36$

_____

21. $x^3 + 4x^2 - 12x$

_____

22. $16y^3 - 22y^2 + 6y$

_____

Apply the Idea

23. A certain style of packing crate comes in different sizes. The volume of each crate can be found using the expression $3x^3 + 10x^2 - 8x$, where x is the measure in feet of one dimension of the crate. (Remember, the formula for volume is Volume = length • width • height.)

    a. What are the measurements of the other two dimensions? _____

    b. What are the dimensions of the crate if one side is 4 feet long? _____

Write About It

24. Try factoring the expression $8x^2 - 16x - 64$ without using the distributive property. Then factor the expression by using the distributive property. Which method did you prefer? What guideline does this suggest for factoring expressions?

_____

_____

_____

_____

_____

_____

_____

10•4 Factoring Differences of Two Squares and Perfect Square Trinomials

IN THIS LESSON, YOU WILL LEARN

To factor a difference of two squares

To factor a perfect square trinomial

WORDS TO LEARN

Difference of two squares *a binomial of the form* $x^2 - y^2$

Perfect square trinomials *polynomials of the form* $x^2 - 2xy + y^2$ *or* $x^2 + 2xy + y^2$

Umi has learned to use several different strumming patterns when she is playing the guitar. She chooses the pattern that complements a song by studying the song's rhythm and tempo. She has noticed that she uses a similar kind of analysis when she solves algebra problems—she can solve the problem easily by noticing common patterns in the terms.

New Idea

The product of two binomials may be a trinomial. However, if two binomials are a sum and difference of the same terms, their product is another binomial.

$$\textbf{Examples:} \quad (x + 2)(x - 2) = x^2 - 2x + 2x - 4$$
$$= x^2 - 4$$

$$(2m + 3)(2m - 3) = 4m^2 - 6m + 6m - 9$$
$$= 4m^2 - 9$$

Both $x^2 - 4$ and $4m^2 - 9$ are examples of a special kind of polynomial. The terms x^2 and 4 are squares. The terms $4m^2$ and 9 are also squares. So each of these polynomials is called a **difference of two squares** (DIHF-uhr-uhns uhv too skwairz).

You can use the following pattern to factor the difference of two squares:

$$x^2 - y^2 = (x + y)(x - y)$$

Examples: Factor $n^2 - 25$.

Both terms are perfect squares:
$n^2 = (n)(n)$ and $25 = (5)(5)$

Use the difference of two squares pattern.

$$n^2 - 25 = (n + 5)(n - 5)$$

Use FOIL to check the answer.

$$(n + 5)(n - 5) = n^2 - 5n + 5n - 25$$
$$= n^2 - 25$$

Factor $16a^8 - b^2$.

Both terms are perfect squares:
$16a^8 = (4a^4)(4a^4)$ and $b^2 = (b)(b)$

Use the difference of two squares pattern.

$$16a^8 - b^2 = (4a^4 + b)(4a^4 - b)$$

Use FOIL to check the answer.

$$(4a^4 + b)(4a^4 - b) = 16a^8 - 4a^4b + 4a^4b - b^2$$
$$= 16a^8 - b^2$$

⤺Remember

When you multiply expressions such as $(4a^4)(4a^4)$, you *add* the exponents.

✓Check Your Understanding

1. Can you use the difference of two squares pattern to factor $4r^2 + 16$? Why or why not?

_____

_____

Focus on the Idea

To factor a difference of two squares, use the pattern
$x^2 - y^2 = (x + y)(x - y)$.

Practice

Factor each difference of two squares. The first one is done for you.

2. $9x^2 - 1$ 3. $25r^2 - 36$

_____ (3x + 1)(3x − 1) _____   _____

4. $a^2 - 100$

5. $x^4 - 49$

_____

_____

6. $144 - y^2$

7. $4a^4 - 9b^2$

_____

_____

8. $4s^4 - 225$

9. $a^8 - b^4$

_____

_____

10. $36x^2y^2 - x^4y^4$

11. $64 - w^4v^2$

_____

_____

Extend the Idea

You can use another pattern to help you factor polynomials that are called **perfect square trinomials** (PER-fihkt skwair try-NOH-mee-uhlz).

Notice what happens when you square a binomial of the form $(x + y)$ or $(x - y)$.

$$(a + 3)^2 = (a + 3)(a + 3)$$
$$= a^2 + 3a + 3a + 9$$
$$= a^2 + 6a + 9$$

$$(s - 4)^2 = (s - 4)(s - 4)$$
$$= s^2 - 4s - 4s + 16$$
$$= s^2 - 8s + 16$$

In both cases, the first term of the trinomial is the square of the first term of the binomial. The middle term of the trinomial is twice the product of the terms of the binomial: $2(a \cdot 3)$ and $2(s \cdot -4)$. The third term of the trinomial is the square of the second term of the binomial.

This proves that the following patterns can be used to factor perfect square trinomials.

$$x^2 + 2xy + y^2 = (x + y)^2$$
$$x^2 - 2xy + y^2 = (x - y)^2$$

Example: Factor the polynomial. $a^2 + 10a + 25$

First, determine if the polynomial is a perfect square trinomial. There are three tests.

- The first term must be a perfect square: $a^2 = (a)(a)$

- The third term must be a perfect square: $25 = (5)(5)$

- The middle term must be twice the product of a and 5: $10a = 2(a \cdot 5)$

The polynomial $a^2 + 10a + 25$ is a perfect square trinomial, where the "x" is a and the "y" is 5.

So, $a^2 + 10a + 25 = (a + 5)^2$.

✓Check the Math

12. A sample problem showed the quadratic expression $g^8 - 18g^4 + 81$ factored as $(g^4 - 9)^2$. Is the expression factored completely? Explain your answer.

_____

Practice

Determine if the polynomial is a perfect square trinomial. If it is, factor it as the square of a binomial. If it is not, write *not a perfect square trinomial.* The first one is done for you.

13. $x^2 - 10x + 25$ 14. $t^2 + 4t + 4$

  $\underline{(x - 5)^2}$ _____

15. $m^2 - 12m + 36$ 16. $4s^2 + 12s + 9$

  _____   _____

17. $16x^2 - 50x + 25$ 18. $4x^2 - 4xy + y^2$

  _____   _____

Apply the Idea

19. Students at East High School grow organic vegetables in a garden with the dimensions 15 ft long by 15 ft wide. They want to expand the garden as shown by the four arrows.

  a. Write an expression that gives the area of the expanded garden. _____

  b. What kind of polynomial is the expression you wrote for part a? _____

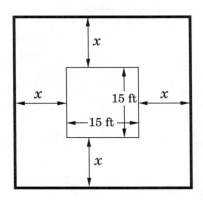

✏ Write About It

20. Give at least two examples of a trinomial that cannot be factored using either of the perfect square trinomials. Explain why they do not fit either pattern.

_____

_____

◢10●5 Zero Products

◢IN THIS LESSON, YOU WILL LEARN

To recognize that if a product of two or more factors is 0, at least one factor is 0

WORDS TO LEARN

Zero Product Property *if the product a • b is equal to 0, then a = 0 or b = 0, or a and b are both equal to 0*

Michael wants to know how much money he will earn per year at his new job. He uses a calculator to multiply his hourly wage, the number of hours he works each week, and the number of weeks he works in a year. The calculator displays a product of 0. What error could Michael have made?

New Idea

You know that $x \cdot 0 = 0$ and that $0 \cdot x = 0$. In general, the product of any number times 0 is 0. You can also reverse this rule: If the product of two numbers is 0, then at least one of those numbers must be 0. This is called the **Zero Product Property** (ZIHR-oh PRAHD-ukt PRAHP-uhr-tee), and it can expressed as follows: If $a \cdot b = 0$, then $a = 0$ or $b = 0$.

You can use the Zero Product Property to solve some equations.

Examples: Solve. $(x + 4)(x - 3) = 0$

The product is 0. Therefore, at least one of the factors must be zero.

$$x + 4 = 0 \qquad \text{or} \qquad x - 3 = 0$$
$$x = -4 \qquad\qquad\qquad x = 3$$

The solution to the equation is $x = -4$ or $x = 3$.

Solve. $y(y + 7) = 0$

At least one factor must be 0.

$$y = 0 \qquad \text{or} \qquad y + 7 = 0$$
$$y = -7$$

The solution is $y = 0$ or $y = -7$.

⌐Remember

The Zero Product Property applies to two or more factors.

Solve. $n(n + 2)(n - 5) = 0$

$$n = 0 \quad \text{or} \quad n + 2 = 0 \quad \text{or} \quad n - 5 = 0$$

$$n = -2 \qquad\qquad n = 5$$

The solution is $n = 0$, $n = -2$, or $n = 5$.

Focus on the Idea

In an equation of the form $a \cdot b = 0$, at least one of the factors must be 0.

Practice

Solve each equation. The first one is done for you.

1. $(x + 5)(x - 5) = 0$

              $x = -5$ or $x = 5$

2. $m(m - 1) = 0$

3. $(v + 5)(v + 6) = 0$

4. $(y + 9)(y - 1) = 0$

5. $(z + 14)(z + 21) = 0$

6. $3x(x - 5) = 0$

7. $(n - 19)(n - 117) = 0$

8. $2x(x + 3)(x - 4) = 0$

9. $48w(w + 1) = 0$

10. $m(m - 6)(m - 7) = 0$

Apply the Idea

11. Write an equation that has the solution $x = -8$ or $x = 6$.

12. Write an equation that has the solution $y = 0$, $y = 4$, or $y = 9$.

Write About It

13. Refer back to Michael's problem at the beginning of this lesson. What errors could Michael have made?

◢10•6 Solving Equations by Factoring

▸IN THIS LESSON, YOU WILL LEARN
To solve quadratic equations that can be factored

WORDS TO LEARN
Quadratic equation *a polynomial equation of the form* $ax^2 + bx + c = 0$

Tiffany is a landscaper. She needs to double the size, or area, of the flower bed shown at the right by adding a border of equal width on three sides. How wide should Tiffany make the border?

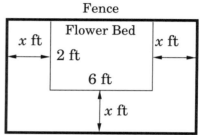

New Idea

A polynomial of the form $ax^2 + bx + c = 0$ is called a **quadratic equation** (kwah-DRAT-ihk ee-KWAY-zhuhn). You may be able to solve a quadratic equation by factoring it and applying the Zero Product Property.

Examples: Solve. $x^2 - 7x - 8 = 0$

Begin by factoring the polynomial on the left side of the equation.

$$(x - 8)(x + 1) = 0$$

According to the Zero Product Property, at least one of the factors, $x - 8$ or $x + 1$, must be 0.

$$x - 8 = 0 \quad \text{or} \quad x + 1 = 0$$
$$x = 8 \qquad\qquad x = -1$$

The solution is $x = 8$ or $x = -1$.

To check the solutions, substitute each one for x in the original equation.

$$x^2 - 7x - 8 = 0 \qquad\qquad x^2 - 7x - 8 = 0$$
$$(8)^2 - (7)(8) - 8 \stackrel{?}{=} 0 \qquad (-1)^2 - (7)(-1) - 8 \stackrel{?}{=} 0$$
$$64 - 56 - 8 \stackrel{?}{=} 0 \qquad\qquad 1 + 7 - 8 \stackrel{?}{=} 0$$
$$0 = 0 \qquad\qquad\qquad 0 = 0$$

How wide should Tiffany make the border around her flower bed?

Tiffany can solve her problem by writing and solving a quadratic equation. The length of the expanded flower bed is $(6 + 2x)$. The width of the expanded flower bed is $(2 + x)$.

The area of the expanded flower bed should be twice the area of the existing flower bed.

$$(6 + 2x)(2 + x) = 2(6 \cdot 2)$$

$$12 + 10x + 2x^2 = (2)(12)$$

$$= 24$$

To solve the equation $12 + 10x + 2x^2 = 24$, rewrite the equation in the form $ax^2 + bx + c = 0$. Then factor the quadratic expression and apply the Zero Product Property.

$$12 + 10x + 2x^2 = 24$$

$-12 + 10x + 2x^2 = 0$ ←Subtract 24 from both sides.

$2x^2 + 10x - 12 = 0$ ←Rewrite in the form $ax^2 + bx + c = 0$.

$2(x^2 + 5x - 6) = 0$ ←Factor out the GCF.

$2(x + 6)(x - 1) = 0$ ←Factor the trinomial.

$(x + 6)(x - 1) = 0$ ←Divide both sides by 2.

$x + 6 = 0$ or $x - 1 = 0$ ←Zero Product Property

$x = -6$ or $x = 1$ ←Solve.

The border cannot be the negative number, -6. So Tiffany should make the border 1 foot wide.

Check: The area of the original flower bed is $(6 \text{ ft})(2 \text{ ft}) = 12 \text{ ft}^2$. The area of the expanded flower bed is $(8 \text{ ft})(3 \text{ ft}) = 24 \text{ ft}^2$. The expanded flower bed is twice the size of the original one.

✓Check Your Understanding

1. What is the first step you would use to solve the equation $21 = 2y + 3y^2$? _____

⬛Focus on the Idea

You can solve some quadratic equations by factoring. It may be necessary to start by rewriting the equation in the form $ax^2 + bx + c = 0$.

Practice

Solve each equation by factoring, if possible. If the equation cannot be solved by factoring, write *cannot be solved by factoring*. The first one is done for you.

2. $x^2 - 3x + 2 = 0$
$(x - 1)(x - 2) = 0$
$x - 1 = 0 \text{ or } x - 2 = 0$
$x = 1 \text{ or } x = 2$

3. $w^2 + 11w + 24 = 0$

4. $y^2 + 6y - 16 = 0$

5. $5x^2 + 2x - 3 = 0$

6. $m^2 = 5m - 6$

7. $2x^2 - x = 10$

8. $3x^2 = 4x + 1$

9. $6 = 13w - 5w^2$

Extend the Idea

You can use what you know about factoring quadratic expressions to solve other kinds of equations. Here is an example of a cubic equation:

$$x^3 + 7x^2 + 6x = 0.$$

Applying the distributive property results in $x(x^2 + 7x + 6) = 0$. Factoring the quadratic expression $x^2 + 7x + 6$ results in $(x)(x + 6)(x + 1) = 0$. The solution is $x = 0$, $x = -6$, or $x = -1$.

✓Check the Math

10. Zach must solve the equation $t^3 - 3t^2 - 28t = 0$. He begins by applying the distributive property so that the equation reads $t(t^2 - 3t - 28) = 0$. Then he factors the quadratic expression to give the equation $t(t - 7)(t + 4) = 0$. Is his work correct? What should he do next?

Practice

Solve each cubic equation.

11. $x^3 - 7x^2 + 12x = 0$

12. $2m^3 = m^2 + m$

13. $y^3 - 4y$

14. $3n^3 - 18n^2 + 27n$

Apply the Idea

15. The length of a rectangular flower bed is 3 feet greater than the width. The flower bed has an area of 108 square feet. Write and solve a quadratic equation to find the dimensions of the flower bed.

   _____

   _____

Write About It

16. **a.** Write a quadratic equation that has the solution $x = 2$ or $x = 6$. _____

   b. Explain how you can work backward from a solution in order to write a quadratic equation that fits the solution.

   _____

   _____

   _____

◢ 10•7 The Quadratic Formula

◢ IN THIS LESSON, YOU WILL LEARN

To use the quadratic formula to solve quadratic equations

WORDS TO LEARN

Quadratic formula *the formula* $x = \dfrac{-b \pm \sqrt{b^2 - 4ac}}{2a}$
that gives the solution to any equation of the form
$ax^2 + bx + c = 0$

Not every polynomial of the form $ax^2 + bx + c$ can be factored. If you try all the possible factors and none work, then the polynomial cannot be factored. In this lesson, you will learn a method for solving any quadratic equation, even those that cannot be factored.

New Idea

The **quadratic formula** (kwah-DRAT-ihk FAWR-myoo-luh) states that if $ax^2 + bx + c = 0$, a is not 0, and $b^2 - 4ac \geq 0$, then
$x = \dfrac{-b \pm \sqrt{b^2 - 4ac}}{2a}$. The quadratic formula can be used to solve any quadratic equation.

The symbol $\pm$, which is read "plus or minus," indicates that there are two values. So 5 ± 3 means $5 + 3$, or 8, and $5 - 3$, or 2, and $x = 3 \pm \sqrt{2}$ means $x = 3 + \sqrt{2}$ and $x = 3 - \sqrt{2}$.

Example: Use the quadratic formula to solve $x^2 = 9 - 2x$.

Start by writing the equation in the form $ax^2 + bx + c = 0$. The equation $x^2 = 9 - 2x$ can be rewritten as $x^2 + 2x - 9 = 0$.

Identify the values for a, b, and c and then substitute them into the quadratic formula.

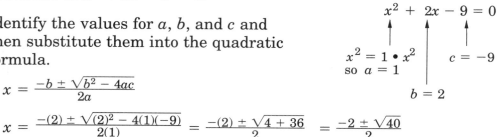

$$x = \frac{-b \pm \sqrt{b^2 - 4ac}}{2a}$$

$$x = \frac{-(2) \pm \sqrt{(2)^2 - 4(1)(-9)}}{2(1)} = \frac{-(2) \pm \sqrt{4 + 36}}{2} = \frac{-2 \pm \sqrt{40}}{2}$$

Use the square root key on your calculator to find the approximate square root of 40.

Because $\sqrt{40} \approx 6.3$, $x \approx \dfrac{-2 \pm 6.3}{2} \approx 2.15$ or -4.15.

Focus on the Idea

You can solve any equation of the form
$ax^2 + bx + c = 0$ by substituting the values for a, b,
and c in the quadratic formula $x = \dfrac{-b \pm \sqrt{b^2 - 4ac}}{2a}$.

Practice

Write the values of a, b, and c for each equation. Then use the
quadratic formula to solve each equation. Estimate square roots to
the nearest tenth. The first one is done for you.

1. $3x^2 - 2x - 2 = 0$

   $a = 3, b = -2, c = -2;$

   $x = \dfrac{-(-2) \pm \sqrt{(-2)^2 - 4(3)(-2)}}{2(3)}$

   $x = \dfrac{2 \pm \sqrt{28}}{6}$

   $x \approx 1.22 \text{ or } -0.55$

2. $w^2 + 6w + 4 = 0$

3. $2r^2 + 5r = -2$

4. $y^2 - 3y - 6 = 0$

5. $6x - 1 = -x^2$

6. $9s = 4 - 2s^2$

Apply the Idea

7. The Pythagorean Theorem states that $a^2 + b^2 = c^2$, where a
   and b are the lengths of the legs of a right triangle and c is
   the length of the side opposite the right angle.

   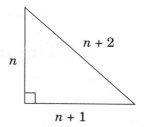

   a. Write a quadratic equation using the Pythagorean
      Theorem for this right triangle.

      _____

   b. Use the quadratic formula to solve the quadratic
      equation you wrote. _____

Write About It

8. What happens to the quadratic formula when $a = 0$?

   _____

   _____

Chapter 10   Review

In This Chapter, You Have Learned

- To find the greatest common factor
- To find the greatest common monomial factor of a polynomial
- To factor quadratic expressions
- To factor a difference of two squares or a perfect square trinomial
- To recognize that if a product of two or more factors is 0, at least one factor is 0
- To solve quadratic equations by factoring or by using the quadratic formula

Words You Know

From the lists of "Words to Learn," choose the word or phrase that best completes each statement.

1. The greatest number that divides two numbers evenly is the _____ of the numbers.

2. According to the _____, if $ax^2 + bx + c = 0$, then $x = \frac{-b \pm \sqrt{b^2 - 4ac}}{2a}$.

3. A polynomial of the form $x^2 - y^2$ is called a(n) _____.

More Practice

Find the greatest common factor of each group.

4. 9, 18, 24

5. 4, 19, 48

6. $8rs,\ 16r,\ 12s$

7. $15x^2y^3,\ 21x^2,\ 24xy$

Factor each polynomial.

8. $18a^5b^2 - 12a^3b^2$

9. $x^2 - 8x - 9$

10. $b^2 - 81$

11. $4y^2 + 6y - 4$

12. $9r^2 - 9r - 10$

13. $25 + 40x + 16x^2$

_____

_____

14. $y^2 - y - 42$

15. $9a^2 - 4b^2$

_____

_____

Solve each equation.

16. $(t + 3)(t + 1) = 0$

17. $x(x - 8) = 0$

_____

_____

18. $(m + 15)(m - 17) = 0$

19. $n(n - 2)(n - 3) = 0$

_____

_____

Solve each equation by factoring.

20. $w^2 - 12w + 11 = 0$

21. $x^2 - x - 20 = 0$

_____

_____

22. $2r^2 + 9r = 35$

23. $-12 = 14y - 10y^2$

_____

_____

Use the quadratic formula to solve each equation.

24. $2r^2 - 8r + 3 = 0$

25. $x^2 + 6x + 4 = 0$

_____

_____

26. $m^2 + 3m = 2$

27. $2x^2 = 3 - 7x$

_____

_____

Problems You Can Solve

28. The length of a rectangle is 6 inches greater than the width. The area of the rectangle is 187 square inches. What are the dimensions of the rectangle?

_____

29. For Your Portfolio Write a word problem that can be solved by finding the greatest common factor of two or more numbers. Use the problem on page 162 as a model if you like.

_____

_____

Chapter 10   Practice Test

Write the greatest common factor of each group.

1. 24, 42, 52

2. $4x^3y^2$, $9x^2y^2$, $12y^2$

Factor each polynomial.

3. $x^2 - 16$

4. $15r^2s + 45r$

5. $y^2 + 14y + 49$

6. $w^2 - w + 72$

7. $a^4 - b^6$

8. $16 - 16y + 4y^2$

9. $12m^2 + 2m - 2$

10. $7a^4b^2 - 4b^2$

Solve each equation.

11. $x(x - 3) = 0$

12. $(a + 4)(a - 5) = 0$

Solve each equation by factoring.

13. $w^2 + 5w - 14 = 0$

14. $6x^2 = 13x - 5$

15. $2y^2 - 2y = 24$

16. $10m^2 + 8 = 24m$

Use the quadratic formula to solve each equation.

17. $x^2 + 3x + 1 = 0$

18. $4z^2 - 5z + 1 = 0$

19. $2n^2 + 8n = -3$

20. $y^2 = 2y + 2$

Chapter 11

Systems of Equations

> **OBJECTIVES:**
>
> **In this chapter, you will learn**
>
> - *To recognize a system of equations*
> - *To write a system of equations*
> - *To find the solution to a system of equations by graphing*
> - *To solve a system of equations by addition or subtraction*
> - *To solve systems of equations using two steps—multiplication and addition*
> - *To solve a system by substituting to eliminate variables*

To solve a mystery, you rearrange and examine related pieces of information to find "who done it." Good mystery writers, like those listed here, always give the reader enough clues to solve the mystery. But no one says it has to be easy! The reader must look at each piece of information to see how it relates to other information. Finally, the reader must think in new ways to find the solution.

Find out the name of a main character (for example, the detective or the spy) associated with each of these famous mystery writers. Ask friends who have read their work, or look in the library.

Throughout your study of algebra, you have been a detective. You have searched for one missing piece of information, or the value for one variable. When there have been two variables, you have discovered two pieces of missing information. This chapter will teach you new ways to solve two equations with two variables.

John Dickson Carr
Raymond Chandler
Agatha Christie
Arthur Conan Doyle
Ian Fleming
Erle Stanley Gardner
Dashiell Hammett
P.D. James
John Le Carré
Ed McBain
Sara Paretsky
Edgar Allen Poe
Dorothy L. Sayers
Dorothy Uhnak

▾**IN THIS LESSON, YOU WILL LEARN**

To write a system of equations

To recognize a system of equations

WORDS TO LEARN

System of equations *two or more equations using the same variables*

Solution set *the set of all solutions that a system of equations has in common*

A legend tells that the tomb of an early Greek mathematician named Diophantus had this riddle carved on it. Each sentence about Diophantus's life can be written as an equation. The equations will produce a common solution to the riddle.

> Diophantus passed $\frac{1}{6}$ of his life in childhood, $\frac{1}{12}$ in youth, and $\frac{1}{7}$ more as a bachelor. Five years after his marriage, a son was born who died four years before his father, at half his fathers total life span. How many years did Diophantus live?

New Idea

Two (or more) equations that contain the same variables form a **system of equations** (SIHS-tuhm, ee-KWAY-zhuhnz). These equations can be solved together to find the set of solutions. Numbers in the **solution set** (suh-LOO-shuhn seht) make all the equations true when you substitute the solutions for the variables.

Example: Are these two equations a system of equations?

$$a = 2b + 7 \qquad 3a = 9b$$

These two equations both have the same variables, a and b. The solution set is $a = 21$ and $b = 7$.

To solve the riddle of Diophantus, write the facts about his life as a system of equations. Let d stand for his life span and s for his age when his son was born.

childhood + youth + bachelorhood + 5 = s

$$\tfrac{1}{6}d + \tfrac{1}{12}d + \tfrac{1}{7}d + 5 \quad = s$$

age of Diophantus when son died − s = son's age

$$(d - 4) - s = \tfrac{1}{2}d$$

The solution set is $d = 84$ and $s = 38$.

Check, by substituting these values into both equations.

$$\tfrac{1}{6}(84) + \tfrac{1}{12}(84) + \tfrac{1}{7}(84) + 5 \stackrel{?}{=} 38$$

$$38 = 38$$

$$(84 - 4) - 38 \stackrel{?}{=} \tfrac{1}{2}(84)$$

$$42 = 42$$

Diophantus lived to be 84, and he was 38 when his son was born.

Focus on the Idea

A system of equations contains two or more equations using the same variables. A system of equations can be solved to find the set of solutions common to all the equations.

Practice

Write *yes* if the equations form a system; otherwise, write *no*. The first one is done for you.

1. $3a + 2b = 7$
$3x + 2y = 7$

_____no_____

2. $2x = 4y + 6$
$3x - y = -1$

_____

3. $5a + 6b + 7c = 38$
$a + b + c = 6$
$abc = 6$

_____

Tell whether ($x = 2$, $y = 3$) is a solution to the set of equations.

4. $x + y = 5$
$2x + y = 10$

_____

5. $2x + 3y = 13$
$7x - 2y = 8$

_____

6. $y = x + 1$
$2y - 7 = -\tfrac{1}{2}x$

_____

Apply the Idea

Write a system of equations for each situation. Do not solve the equations.

7. Juan is 4 years older than his brother. The sum of their ages is 36.

_____

8. Three magazines and two cards cost $11. Two magazines and three cards cost $9.

_____

Write About It

9. Write a problem using your age and the age of another family member. Write two equations to solve your problem.

_____

_____

↰**IN THIS LESSON, YOU WILL LEARN**

To find the solution of a system of equations by graphing

WORDS TO LEARN

Graphing method *to solve a system of equations by graphing*

Maria has two puppies she is raising as show dogs. She keeps careful track of their weights. Bubbles weighs 11 pounds and is gaining 2 pounds a week. Streak weighs 8 pounds and is gaining 3 pounds a week. If they keep growing at these rates, how many weeks will it be before the puppies are the same weight?

New Idea

You can find the solution set of a system of equations by graphing. This is called the **graphing method** (GRAF-ihng MEHTH-uhd). Graph the line described by each equation. The coordinates of the point the lines have in common is their common solution, or the solution set for the equations.

↪*Remember*

To graph the equation of a line, make a table of ordered pairs. To find ordered pairs, select a value for one variable and substitute that value in the equation to find the value for the other variable. Locate the points for each ordered pair on the coordinate plane. Then join the points with a line. The line shows the complete solution set of the equation.

Example: Use the graphing method to find the solution to the question about Maria's puppies.

First write an equation for each growth rate. Let w stand for the number of weeks of growth and p for the final weight.

$$11 + 2w = p \qquad \leftarrow \text{Bubbles}$$

$$8 + 3w = p \qquad \leftarrow \text{Streak}$$

Then find at least three sets of ordered pairs that satisfy each equation.

$$11 + 2w = p \qquad 8 + 3w = p$$

w	p
0	11
1	13
2	15
3	17

w	p
0	8
1	11
2	14
3	17

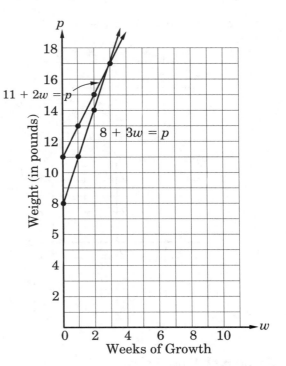

Finally, graph the ordered pairs. Draw and label each line.

The lines cross at (3, 17). This means that, after 3 weeks, the puppies each weigh 17 pounds.

✓ **Check Your Understanding**

1. Find three ordered pairs that satisfy the equation $x + 7 = y$.

◀ Focus on the Idea

To solve a system of equations, graph a line for each equation. The point at which the lines intersect is the common solution, or the solution set.

Practice

Solve the system of equations by graphing. Find at least three ordered pairs for each equation. Then graph them on the coordinate plane. The first one is done for you.

2. $3x - 2 = y \qquad 2x - 1 = y$

x	y
0	-2
1	1
2	4

x	y
0	-1
1	1
2	3

3. $x - 2 = y \qquad -2x + 1 = y$

x	y

x	y

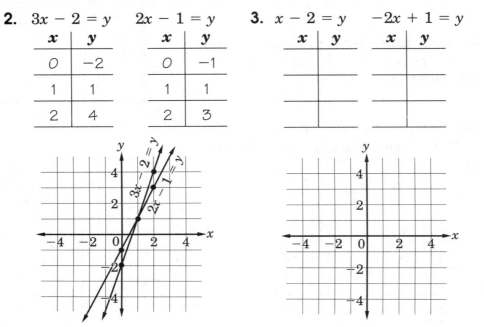

4. $x + y = 5$ $\quad x - y = 1$

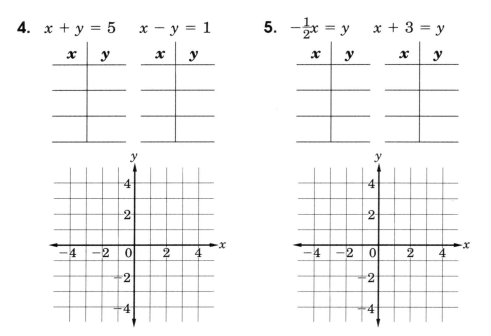

5. $-\frac{1}{2}x = y$ $\quad x + 3 = y$

x	y

x	y

x	y

x	y

Extend the Idea

A system of equations may produce two parallel lines. This means there is no solution set. If the lines coincide, every point on the line is a solution to both equations, so the solution set is infinite.

Examples: Solve the following system of equations by using the graphing method: $m = 5t$ and $m = 5t + 1$.

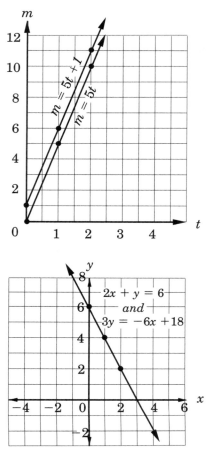

$m = 5t$

t	m
0	0
1	5
2	10

$m = 5t + 1$

t	m
0	1
1	6
2	11

Notice that the lines are parallel and so will never cross. Thus, there is no solution to the system.

Use the graphing method to solve this system of equations: $2x + y = 6$ and $3y = -6x + 18$.

$2x + y = 6$ $\quad 3y = -6x + 18$

x	y
0	6
1	4
2	2

x	y
0	6
1	4
2	2

The graphs of these two equations, $2x + y = 6$ and $3y = -6x + 18$, are exactly the same line, so there is an infinite number of solutions for this system.

✓ Check the Math

6. Sophie had to solve the system of equations: $x + y = 3$ and $3x + 3y = 9$. She said, "I know they have an infinite number of solutions." Explain how she knew this without graphing.

_____

Practice

Solve the system of equations by graphing.

7. $2x = y$ $3y = 6x + 1$

8. $2x + 2y = -2$ $3x + 3y = -3$

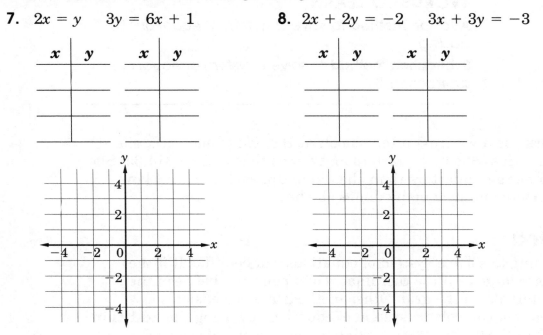

Apply the Idea

9. Ken skates on the path along the river. He travels at 12 miles per hour. Isaac runs the same path at 8 miles per hour. On Saturday, Ken starts 1 hour after Isaac. When will he overtake Isaac? _____

✎ Write About It

10. How could graphing be used to solve a system of three or four equations? Explain your answer.

_____

_____

_____

▼**IN THIS LESSON, YOU WILL LEARN**
To solve a system of equations by addition or subtraction

WORDS TO LEARN
Addition method *to solve a system of equations by adding*
Subtraction method *to solve a system of equations by subtracting*

Sarah works as a waitress after school. At the end of one shift, she counted her tips. She had quarters and dimes that totaled $14.65. She had $1.85 more in quarters than she did in dimes. Figure out how many quarters and how many dimes she had.

New Idea

Graphing to solve a system of equations can be difficult if the numbers are large or if the coordinates of a point fall between the marked intervals on the grid. Other methods may be easier. Sometimes, you can solve a system of equations by using the **addition method** (uh-DIHSH-uhn MEHTH-uhd) to eliminate one of the variables.

Examples: Solve this system of equations.
$2x + 3y = 16$ and $3x - 3y = -6$

Start by writing the equations in vertical form, aligning like variables.

$$\begin{aligned} 2x + 3y &= 16 \\ +3x - 3y &= -6 \\ \hline 5x + 0 &= 10 \\ \frac{5x}{5} &= \frac{10}{5} \\ x &= 2 \end{aligned}$$ ←Add the two equations.

To find the value of y, substitute 2 for x in either one of the original equations.

$$\begin{aligned} 2x + 3y &= 16 \\ 2(2) + 3y &= 16 \end{aligned}$$ ←Substitute 2 for x.

$$4 + 3y = 16 \quad \leftarrow\text{Simplify.}$$
$$4 - 4 + 3y = 16 - 4 \quad \leftarrow\text{Subtract 4 from both sides.}$$
$$3y = 12 \quad \leftarrow\text{Solve for } y.$$
$$y = 4$$

The solution set to the system of equations is $x = 2$ and $y = 4$.
Check your solutions by substituting them into the other equation.

$$3x - 3y = -6$$
$$3(2) - 3(4) \overset{?}{=} -6$$
$$-6 = -6$$

✓Check the Math

1. Wanda added the system of equations $x + y = 6$ and $x - y = 10$ to get the solution set $x = 8$ and $y = 2$. Is her solution correct? Explain your answer.

_____

◀ Focus on the Idea

To solve a system of equations using addition, write the equations in vertical form. If two coefficients of the same variable have opposite values, add. Solve to find the value of the remaining variable. Then substitute that value in either of the original equations to find the value of the other variable. Check your solutions in the other original equation.

Practice

Solve the systems of equations, using addition. Check your answers in the original equations. The first one is done for you.

2. $\begin{aligned} 2y &= 5x + 8 \\ -2y &= x - 2 \\ \hline 0 &= 6x + 6 \\ -6 &= 6x \\ -1 &= x \end{aligned}$ $\begin{aligned} 2y &= 5(-1) + 8 \\ 2y &= -5 + 8 \\ 2y &= 3 \\ y &= \frac{3}{2} \end{aligned}$ Check: $-2(\frac{3}{2}) \overset{?}{=} -1 - 2$
$$-3 = -3$$

The solution set is $x = -1$ and $y = \frac{3}{2}$.

3. $\begin{aligned} 8x + 5y &= 36 \\ 16x - 5y &= 12 \end{aligned}$

4. $x + 3 = y$
   $-x - 15 = -2y$

5. $x - 4y = -3$
   $x + 4y = 12$

6. $4x + 2y = 17$
   $3x - 2y = 11$

Extend the Idea

If a system of equations has no coefficients that are opposites, you sometimes can use the **subtraction method** (sub-TRAHK-shun MEHTH-uhd) to eliminate one of the variables.

Example: Solve this system of equations.
$x - 3y = 18$ and $x + 5y = 2$

Start by writing the equations in vertical form, aligning like variables.

$$
\begin{array}{rl}
x - 3y = 18 & \\
\underline{-(x + 5y = 2)} & \leftarrow\text{Subtract.} \\
0 - 8y = 16 & \leftarrow\text{Solve for } y. \\
\dfrac{-8y}{-8} = \dfrac{16}{-8} & \\
y = -2 &
\end{array}
$$

To find the value of x, substitute -2 for y in one of the original equations.

$$
\begin{array}{r}
x - 3y = 18 \\
x - 3(-2) = 18 \\
x = 12
\end{array}
$$

The solution set is $x = 12$ and $y = -2$. Check by substituting your solutions into the other equation.

$$
\begin{array}{r}
x + 5y = 2 \\
12 + 5(-2) \stackrel{?}{=} 2 \\
2 = 2
\end{array}
$$

7. Would you use the addition or subtraction method to solve this system of equations? $-4y = x - 3$ and $x + 3y = -9$ Explain your answer.

_____

Practice

Solve, using subtraction. Check your answers.

8. $x + y = 4$
   $x - 5y = -2$

9. $x + 1 = -2y$
   $x - 2 = 3y$

10. $x - y = 5$
    $x + 3y = 17$

11. $4x - 2y = 14$
    $3x - 2y = 11$

Apply the Idea

Answer the question by writing two equations and solving the system with addition or subtraction.

12. Refer to the problem about Sarah's tips on page 192. How many quarters and dimes did she have? _____

13. Maria and Tina shopped together. Tina spent $58 for two T-shirts and a pair of jeans. Maria bought six of the same T-shirts and an identical pair of jeans for $118. What was the price of each item? _____

⟋ Write About It

14. Count the change you have with you. Make up a problem about the number of each kind of coin. Exchange problems with a classmate. Solve each other's problems, using a system of equations.

_____

_____

_____

◢**IN THIS LESSON, YOU WILL LEARN**

To solve systems of equations using two steps— multiplication and addition or multiplication and subtraction

WORDS TO LEARN

Multiplication method *to solve a system of equations, using multiplication before adding or subtracting*

Samantha runs a catering business. She uses different combinations of meats and cheeses to make her appetizers. One pound of meat and 4 pounds of cheese make one kind of appetizer and cost $7. Another kind of appetizer uses 2 pounds of meat and 3 pounds of cheese for $9. How much is Samantha spending on meat and cheese if she makes both kinds of appetizers?

New Idea

Sometimes a system of equations is not easy to solve with graphing, addition, or subtraction. You can use the **multiplication method** (mul-tuh-plih-KAY-shuhn MEHTH-uhd), multiplying before you add or subtract, to solve this kind of system of equations.

Examples: Use a system of equations to answer Samantha's question.

If m represents the cost of the meat and c represents the cost of the cheese, these two equations represent Samantha's costs.

$$m + 4c = 7$$
$$2m + 3c = 9$$

◝*Remember*

Multiplying each side of an equation by the same number leaves the equation unchanged.

Multiply the first equation by 2 to make the coefficients of the terms with m the same.

$$2(m + 4c = 7) = 2m + 8c = 14$$

$$2m + 8c = 14$$
$$-(2m + 3c = 9) \quad \leftarrow\text{Subtract.}$$
$$0 + 5c = 5 \quad \leftarrow\text{Solve for } c.$$
$$c = 1$$

To find the value of m, substitute 1 for c in the second equation.

$$2m + 3c = 9$$
$$2m + 3(1) = 9$$
$$2m = 6$$
$$m = 3$$

Check. $m + 4c = 7$
$$3 + 4(1) \stackrel{?}{=} 7$$
$$7 = 7$$

Samantha pays \$3 for meat and \$1 for cheese.

Solve this system of equations.
$$5x + 3y = 27 \text{ and } 2x - y = 2$$

Notice the coefficients of y. To eliminate y, multiply the second equation by 3.

$$5x + 3y = 27$$
$$3(2x - y = 2) \text{ becomes } \underline{6x - 3y = 6} \quad \leftarrow\text{Add the two equations.}$$
$$11x + 0 = 33 \quad \leftarrow\text{Solve for } x.$$

$$x = 3$$

To solve for y, substitute 3 for x in either original equation.

For the second: $2x - y = 2$
$$2(3) - y = 2 \quad \leftarrow\text{Solve for } y.$$
$$y = 4$$

Check. $5x + 3y = 27$
$$5(3) + 3(4) \stackrel{?}{=} 27$$
$$15 + 12 \stackrel{?}{=} 27$$
$$27 = 27$$

Focus on the Idea

You can use multiplication to solve a system of equations. Multiply one equation by the number that will make the coefficients of a variable either the same or opposite in both equations. Then add or subtract to eliminate that variable.

Practice

Solve each system of equations, using the multiplication method.
Check your answer in the original equations. The first one is done
for you.

1. $x + y = 15$
$3x - 2y = 15$

$2x + 2y = 30$
$\underline{3x - 2y = 15}$
$5x \qquad = 45$
$\qquad x = 9$

$x + y = 15$
$9 + y = 15$
$\qquad y = 6$
$x = 9$ and $y = 6$

2. $y = 3x - 4$
$4y = 9x + 5$

3. $3x + 9 = 9y$
$x - 7 = 2y$

4. $2x + 3y = 11$
$4x + 5y = 19$

5. $x + 5y = 31$
$2x - y = 7$

6. $-2x - 3y = 2$
$3x + y = 10$

Extend the Idea

Often, there is more than one way to solve a system of equations.
Sometimes, multiplying just one equation will not lead to a solution.
You can find the least common multiple (LCM) of two coefficients of
the same variable and then multiply both equations to get the LCM
as the coefficients.

Example: Solve. $2x - 3y = 8$ and $5x + 4y = -3$

The LCM of 3 and 4 is 12, so multiply to change the
coefficients of the y terms to 12.

$$4(2x - 3y = 8) \quad \rightarrow \quad 8x - 12y = 32$$
$$3(5x + 4y = -3) \rightarrow \underline{15x + 12y = -9} \leftarrow \text{Add.}$$
$$23x + \quad 0 = 23 \leftarrow \text{Solve for } x.$$
$$x = 1$$

$$2x - 3y = 8 \quad \leftarrow \text{Substitute 1 for } x.$$
$$2(1) - 3y = 8$$
$$-3y = 6$$
$$y = -2$$

Check. $\quad 5x + 4y = -3 \leftarrow$ Substitute 1 for x
$$5(1) + 4(-2) \stackrel{?}{=} -3 \qquad \text{and } -2 \text{ for } y.$$
$$-3 = -3$$

The solution is $x = 1$ and $y = -2$.

7. By what numbers could you multiply each of these equations to get a common coefficient for the x terms? $3x + 3y = 9$ and $2x - 2y = 2$ _____

Practice

Solve the system of equations. The first one is done for you.

8. $6x - 5y = 1$
$4x - 3y = 3$

$18x - 15y = 3$
$\underline{-20x + 15y = -15}$
$-2x + 0 = -12$
$x = 6$
$6(6) - 5y = 1$
$-5y = -35$
$y = 7$
x = 6 and y = 7

9. $3y = -x + 5$
$2y = -5x - 4$

10. $3x = 7y + 2$
$7x = 12y - 4$

11. $2y = 5x + 13$
$3y = 2x + 18$

12. $4y = -3x + 15$
$-y = 2x - 5$

13. $2y = 4x + 2$
$5y = 9x + 7$

Apply the Idea

14. Henry is making a new 100-pound batch of Special Brew Coffee by mixing Valley Vanilla and Mountain Mist beans. Valley Vanilla beans sell for $8 a pound. Mountain Mist sells for $12 a pound. How many pounds of each must he mix to make Special Brew, which sells for $9 a pound? _____

✐ Write About It

15. Explain the relationship between solving a system of equations and answering a question or problem.

_____

_____

_____

◀11•5 Solving a System of Equations Using Substitution

◀**IN THIS LESSON, YOU WILL LEARN**

To solve a system by substituting to eliminate one variable

WORDS TO LEARN

Substitution method *to solve a system of equations by substituting to get one equation with one variable*

At the subway station, 12 tokens sell for $9 and a monthly pass costs $30. The pass can be used for an unlimited number of rides during the month. Ozzie wants to know which is the better buy, the tokens or the pass. How often would he need to take the subway during a 30-day month for the pass to be a better buy?

New Idea

Sometimes, a system of equations can be solved most easily using the **substitution method** (sub-stuh-TOO-shuhn MEHTH-uhd). First, solve one of the equations for one variable in terms of the other variable. Then substitute that expression in the second equation.

Examples: Write a system of two equations for the subway problem. Let c stand for the cost of a ride using the tokens, and let r stand for the number of rides in a month. The two equations are $9 = 12c$ and $30 = rc$.

$$9 = 12c \qquad \leftarrow \text{Solve the first equation for } c.$$

$$\frac{9}{12} = \frac{12c}{12}$$

$$0.75 = c$$

$$30 = rc \qquad \leftarrow \text{Substitute 0.75 for } c \text{ in the second equation.}$$

$$30 = 0.75r \qquad \leftarrow \text{Solve for } r.$$

$$40 = r$$

At 40 rides per month, the tokens and the pass will cost the same (75 cents). If Ozzie rides more than 40 times in a month, he will save money with a pass.

Solve this system of equations by the substitution method. $3x - y = 4$ and $3y = 24$

$$3x - y = 4$$
$$3y = 24 \qquad \leftarrow \text{Solve for } y.$$
$$y = 8$$
$$3x - 8 = 4 \qquad \leftarrow \text{Substitute 8 for } y \text{ in the first equation.}$$
$$3x = 12 \qquad \leftarrow \text{Solve for } x.$$
$$x = 4$$

Check. $\quad 3x - y = 4$
$$3(4) - 8 \overset{?}{=} 4$$
$$4 = 4$$

✓Check Your Understanding

1. What would be your first step in solving this system of equations with the substitution method? $y = 4x$ and $5y - x = 38$ _____

◣Focus on the Idea

To solve a system of equations by substituting, solve one of the equations for one variable in terms of the other variable. Then substitute the value for that variable in the second equation. Solve to find the value of the second variable.

Practice

Solve each system of equations, using substitution. The first one is done for you.

2. $x + 2y = 4$
   $3x - y = 5$
$$x = 4 - 2y$$
$$3(4 - 2y) - y = 5$$
$$12 - 6y - y = 5$$
$$- 7y = -7$$
$$y = 1$$
$$x + 2y = 4$$
$$x + 2(1) = 4$$
$$x = 2$$
$$x = 2 \text{ and } y = 1.$$
Check. $\quad x + 2y = 4$
$$2 + 2(1) \overset{?}{=} 4$$
$$4 = 4$$

3. $x - y = 6$
   $x + 3y = -2$

4. $x - y = 5$
$\quad 2x + y = 15$

5. $x + 2y = 10$
$\quad 3x - 4y = -10$

6. $3x + 2y = -8$
$\quad 8x - y = -15$

7. $3y = 9x + 12$
$\quad 5y = 23x + 12$

Extend the Idea

Some systems of equations take many steps to solve. However, the method for solving this kind of equation system uses the same processes that you already know. Just follow all the steps you have learned in this chapter.

Example: Solve this system of equations by addition, subtraction, division, substitution, and multiplication.

$$2x - 6y = 16 \quad \leftarrow \text{equation 1}$$
$$5x + 2y = 6 \quad \leftarrow \text{equation 2}$$

Step 1 Solve for x in equation 1.

$$2x - 6y = 16$$
$$2x - 6y + (6y) = 16 + (6y)$$
$$2x = 16 + (6y)$$
$$\frac{2x}{2} = \frac{16 + (6y)}{2}$$
$$x = 8 + 3y$$

Step 2 Substitute your new value of x and solve for y in the second equation.

$$5(8 + 3y) + 2y = 6 \quad \leftarrow \text{Substitute } (8 + 3y) \text{ for } x.$$
$$40 + 15y + 2y = 6$$
$$40 + 17y = 6$$
$$(-40) + 40 + 17y = (-40) + 6$$
$$17y = -34$$
$$y = -2$$

Step 3 Now substitute your new value of y and solve for x in the first equation

$x = 8 + 3y$ from Step 1.
$x = 8 + 3(-2)$ $\leftarrow$ Substitute (-2) for y.
$x = 8 + -6$
$x = 2$

Step 4 In this system, $x = 2$ and $y = -2$. Substitute your values to check.

Check

$2x - 6y = 16$ $\leftarrow$ first equation
$2(2) - 6(-2) \stackrel{?}{=} 16$
$4 - (-12) \stackrel{?}{=} 16$
$16 = 16$

$5x + 2y = 6$ $\leftarrow$ second equation
$5(2) + 2(-2) \stackrel{?}{=} 6$
$10 + (-4) \stackrel{?}{=} 6$
$6 = 6$

✓ Check the Math

8. Sam said that the easier way to solve this system, $x - y = 7$ and $3x - 4y = 19$, is by solving for x in the first equation. Sari said it would be easier to solve for y in the second equation. Who is right? Why?

_____

Practice

Solve for both variables. Part of the first one is done for you.

9. $2y = 4x + 1$
$6y = 10x - 3$
$2y = 4x + 1$
$y = 2x + \frac{1}{2}$

10. $5x + 3y = 55$
$3x + y = 25$

Apply the Idea

11. The length of Community Park is three times its width. The perimeter of the park is 640 feet. Find the length and width of the park. _____

✏ Write About It

12. Which method of solving a system of equations do you think is best: graphing, addition, subtraction, multiplication, or substitution? Explain your answer.

_____

Chapter 11   Review

In This Chapter, You Have Learned

- To recognize a system of equations
- To write a system of equations
- To find the solution of a system of equations by graphing
- To solve a system of equations by addition or subtraction
- To solve systems of equations using two steps—multiplication and addition or multiplication and subtraction
- To solve a system by substituting to eliminate one variable

Words You Know

From the lists of "Words to Learn," choose the word or phrase that best completes each statement.

1. Two or more equations using the same variables are a(n) _____.

2. _____ is the set of numbers that makes a system of equations true.

3. The three ways of solving a system of equations are _____, _____, _____.

More Practice

Write *yes* for a system of equations; otherwise write *no*.

4. $6a - b = 7$
    $a + b = 14$ _____

5. $8x = 4y + 6$
    $2x - y = 1$ _____

Tell whether ($x = 4$, $y = -1$) is a solution of these systems of equations.

6. $x - y = 5$
    $2x + y = 10$ _____

7. $3x - y = 13$
    $-2x - 3y = -5$ _____

Solve each system of equations by graphing.

8. $4x + y = 11$
    $y = x + 1$

9. $x + 3 = y$
    $-2x + 6 = y$

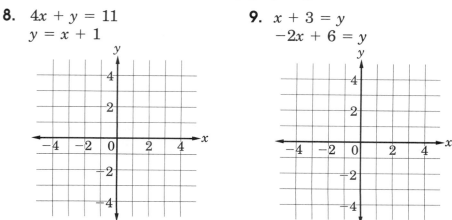

Solve each system of equations, using addition or subtraction.

10. $4y = 5x + 5$
$y = 5x - 5$

11. $6y = 2x + 7$
$5y = -2x + 15$

Solve each system of equations, using the multiplication method.

12. $6x - 5y = 1$
$4x - 3y = 3$

13. $9y = x - 12$
$-2y = 3x + 14$

Solve each system of equations, using the substitution method.

14. $x + y = 20$
$3x - 2y = 20$

15. $3y = -x + 5$
$2y = -5x - 4$

Problems You Can Solve

Write a system of equations for each. Then solve.

16. Three times a number x minus 4 equals another number, y. The sum of the numbers is 12. Find the numbers.

_____

17. Six marigold plants and two packages of zinnia seeds cost $14. Two marigold plants and six packages of zinnia seeds cost $10. Find the price of a plant and of a package of seeds.

_____

18. Nathaniel found some quarters and dimes in the sofa that were worth $3. The quarters were worth $2 more than the dimes. How many quarters did he find?

_____

19. Nigel has 18 CDs more than Robin. Together they have 48 CDs. How many CDs does each have?

_____

20. For Your Portfolio Determine the rate at which you perform a certain activity. For example, find the rate at which you read, bike, skate, type, travel to school, or commute to your job. Write an equation for the rate, and graph the equation. Then determine how you could improve that rate by changing one of the variables, such as the length of time you do the activity. Write another equation and graph it. Compare the graphs.

_____

_____

_____

Chapter 11 Practice Test

Tell whether $(-1, -2)$ is a solution to the system of equations.

1. $x + y = -3$
   $3x - 3y = 3$ _____

Solve each system of equations by graphing.

2. $x = y$
   $-2x = y$

3. $x + 1 = y$
   $-2x - 8 = y$

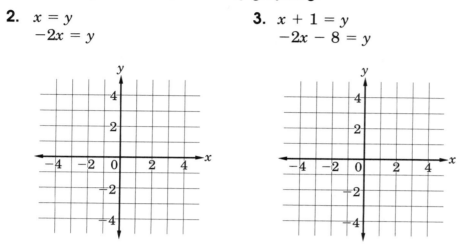

Solve the system of equations, using addition or subtraction.

4. $9y = 3x - 36$
   $-y = 3x + 24$

5. $y = 2x - 9$
   $-y = 3x - 11$

Solve each system of equations, using the multiplication method.

6. $-2x + 5y = 1$
   $5x - 2y = 8$

7. $7x = 5y - 6$
   $4x = 3y - 5$

Solve each system of equations, using the substitution method.

8. $-x + 6 = y$
   $7x + 8 = -2y$

9. $2x + 9y = 36$
   $x - 2y = 5$

Solve.

10. Nine pairs of socks and a pair of gym shoes cost $72. Five pairs of socks cost one third as much as a pair of gym shoes. Find the price of each.

Glossary

A

Absolute value the distance between a number and zero on a number line (4•3)

Absolute-value equation an equation that involves the absolute value of a variable (6•4)

Algebraic sentence a statement that contains numbers or variables (3•1)

Algebraic symbols another term for mathematical symbols (1•6)

Associative Property states that the way in which numbers are grouped does not change the sum or product (2•2)

Axes two perpendicular number lines that meet at their zero points (5•1)

B

Base a number (or variable) multiplied by itself (1•2)

Binomial a polynomial with two terms (9•1)

Blood type a characteristic of blood that is determined by the presence or absence of certain kinds of proteins in the blood (3•7)

Blueprint a diagram showing the shape and measurements of an object (3•3)

Brackets another grouping symbol (1•3)

Budget a listing of fixed expenses that must be paid out of monthly income (8•3)

C

Coefficient the numerical part of a term that is not an exponent (2•1)

Combine like terms to use the distribution property to simplify an expression that contains like terms (2•1)

Commutative Property states that the order in which numbers are added or multiplied does not change the sum or product (2•2)

Continuous graph a graph that can be drawn without lifting the pencil off the page (5•4)

Coordinates the two numbers used to locate a point on a coordinate plane (5•1)

Coordinate plane a region formed by a pair of axes (5•1)

Cube

Cube the multiplication of a factor by itself two times to form a product (7•1)

Cube root a number whose cube equals a given number (7•7)

D

Degree of a term the sum of the exponents of the variables in the term (9•1)

Degree of polynomial the greatest of the degrees of the terms of a polynomial (9•1)

Discrete graph a graph that contains gaps (5•4)

Distributive Property of Multiplication Over Addition states that a product can be found by adding, then multiplying, or by multiplying, then adding (2•3)

E

Elevation the distance above or below seal level (4•7)

Equation a sentence that contains an equal sign (3•1)

Evaluate find the value of an expression (1•1)

Exponent the number of times a base is multiplied by itself (1•2)

Exponential expressions expressions with numbers or variables using exponents (7•3)

Exponential form a number (or variable) written as a base and an exponent (1•2)

Exponential growth a quantity that grows by a power of the original quantity (7•4)

F

Factor a number multiplied by another number to produce a product (2•3)

Financial costs the charges the bank adds to the cost of borrowing money to cover its expenses (3•2)

FOIL method a procedure used for multiplying two binomials (9•4)

Formula an equation that gives the relationship between two or more variables (3•6)

G

Graph of an equation the set of points whose coordinates make an equation true (5•3)

I

Identity Property describes the results of adding 0 to a number or multiplying a number by 1 (2•2)

Improper fraction a fraction whose numerator is greater than or equal to its denominator (3•7)

Inequality a mathematical sentence comparing or ordering two unequal numbers (4•4)

Inequality symbols symbols ($<$, $\leq$, $>$, $\geq$) that show the relationship between equality expressions (8•1)

Integers numbers in the set consisting of all whole numbers and their opposites $\{..., -2, -1, 0, 1, 2, 3, ...\}$ (4•1)

Inverse operations operations that reverse the results of other operations (1•5)

Inverting interchanging the numerator and the denominator of a fraction (3•4)

L

Like terms terms whose variable parts are the same (2•1)

Linear equation an equation whose graph is a straight line (5•3)

M

Mathematical operations addition, subtraction, multiplication, or division of numbers and variables (1•4)

Mixed number the combination of a whole number and a fraction (3•7)

Monomial a term that is a number, a variable, or the product of a number and one or more variables (2•6)

Multiplicative inverse a number times its multiplicative inverse equals 1 (3•4)

Multiplicative Property of Zero states that any number multiplied by 0 has a product of 0 (2•2)

N

Nanosecond one-billionth of a second (7•5)

Negative integer an integer less than zero (4•1)

Number line a diagram with numbers shown as points (4•2)

O

Open sentence an equation that contains a variable (3•1)

Operation addition, subtraction, multiplication, or division of numbers and variables (1•4)

Opposites two numbers that are the same distance from zero on a number line, but in opposite directions (4•1)

Ordered pair two numbers that tell the x-coordinate and the y-coordinate of a point (5•2)

Origin the point at which the x-axis and the y-axis meet at right angles (5•2)

P

Parabola the graph of a quadratic equation of the form $y = ax^2 + bx + c$ (6•5)

Parallel lines lines in the same plane that never cross or intersect (6•5)

Parentheses a grouping symbol (1•3)

Perfect square a number whose square root is a whole number (7•7)

Perpendicular lines lines that intersect to form a right angle (6•5)

Polynomial an algebraic expression made up of one or more terms (9•1)

Positive integers an integer greater than zero (4•1)

Property a rule involving an operation on numbers (2•2)

Proportion an expression that states that two ratios are equal (3•5)

Pythagorean Theorem in a right triangle, the square of the hypotenuse is equal to the sum of the squares of the lengths of the two legs (7•7)

Q

Quadrants the four regions into which a coordinate plane is divided; the axes are not part of the quadrants (5•1)

Quadratic equation an equation in the form of $ax^2 + by + c = 0$ (10•6)

R

Radical symbol the symbol $\sqrt{}$, which indicates a square root (7•7)

Rate a ratio of two measurements expressed in different units (6•1)

Rate of change the ratio that expresses the change in one quantity in relation to the change in another quantity (6•1)

Ratio a comparison of two numbers by division (3•5)

Ray part of a line that starts at one point and extends in one direction (8•1)

Repeated subtraction a method for dividing that involves counting how many times one number can be subtracted from another (7•6)

Revenue the total income of a business or organization (4•6)

S

Salvage to recover a wrecked ship or the contents of the ship (4•8)

Scientific notation a number written as the product of a number greater than or equal to one and less than ten, and a power of ten (7•2)

Sea level the average level of the surfaces of the oceans on earth (4•7)

Sign an indication that a number is left (−) or right (+) of zero on the number line (4•5)

Simplify to perform as many operations on a variable expression as possible (2•4)

Simplify a polynomial to combine the like terms of a polynomial (9•2)

Slope the measure of the steepness of a line (5•5)

Slope-intercept form a linear equation written in the form $y = mx + b$ (6•2)

Solution the value of a variable that makes an open sentence true (3•1)

Square the multiplication of a factor by itself to form a product (7•1)

Square root a number whose square equals a given number (7•7)

Standard form a linear equation written in the form $Ax + By = C$ (6•3)

T

Terms the parts of a variable expression separated by addition or subtraction signs (2•1)

Tolerance range of error a measurement can have and still be correct (8•2)

Trinomial a polynomial with three terms (9•1)

U

Unlike terms terms whose variable parts are not the same (2•1)

V

Variables letters used to represent one or more numbers (1•1)

Variable expressions expressions that include variables, numbers, and mathematical symbols (1•1)

Vinculum a grouping symbol used to show division (1•3)

W

Whole numbers numbers in the set {0, 1, 2, 3, 4, ...} (4•1)

X

x-axis horizontal number line on a coordinate plane (5•2)

x-coordinate a point that is right or left of the origin (5•2)

x-intercept the x-coordinate of the point where a line intersects the x-axis (5•6)

Y

y-axis vertical number line on a coordinate plane (5•2)

y-coordinate a point that is up or down from the origin (5•2)

y-intercept the y-coordinate of a point where a line intersects the y-axis (5•6)

Answers

Chapter 1 The Language of Algebra

1•1 Understanding Variables and Expressions

1. **a.** 1800 **b.** Yes. Writing the number and variable next to each other is another way to represent multiplication, so 150 • n will have the same value as 150n.

3. 8 **5.** 15 **7.** 1 **9.** 3

11. **a.** Yes. Multiplying 6 and h represents what the total pay will be. Subtracting 9 will show Donna's pay after her taxes have been deducted.
b. $28.50

1•2 Understanding Exponents

1. $2 • 2 • 2 • 2$ **3.** 6^4 **5.** 12^3 **7.** 8.5^2 **9.** $10 • 10$
11. $3 • 3 • 3 • 3 • 3 • 3$ **13.** 97 **15.** $6 • 6 • 6$
17. 81 **19.** 2^{13}

1•3 Using Grouping Symbols

1. $(44 - 4) • 4 • 2 = 320$, whereas $44 - (4 • 4 • 2) = 12$
3. $3 + 4$ **5.** $a + b$ **7.** $16 - 9$
9. **a.** 6 **b.** 26 **11.** 77 **13.** 251 **15.** 20
17. Possible answer: $6 - (4 + 2)$

1•4 Understanding Order of Operations

1. Division **3.** Addition **5.** Division
7. 10 **9.** 24 **11.** 19 **13.** 5 **15.** 15
17. $(2 + 5) • 2$ **19.** $(12 + 20) ÷ 4 - 5$
21. $4 • 6 + 7 • 6 - 2 • 3$; $60

1•5 Using Inverse Operations

1. Subtraction; addition **3.** Multiplication; division
5. Division **7.** Multiplication
9. Multiplication and addition
11. **a.** 30 **b.** Multiply 30 taxis by 4 tires each to see if this gives 120 tires.

1•6 Verbal Expressions and Algebraic Expressions

1. • or ( ) **3.** − **5.** $p ÷ 2$ **7.** $\frac{d}{5}$ **9.** $(x + y) ÷ 5$

Chapter 1 Review

1. variable **2.** evaluate **3.** exponent
4. parentheses; brackets; vinculum
5. 7 **6.** 3 **7.** 7^3 **8.** b^5 **9.** $12 • 12 • 12 • 12$
10. $d • d$ **11.** 16 **12.** 1,000 **13.** 625 **14.** 9.6 **15.** 0
16. 6 **17.** 16 **18.** 3 **19.** 4 **20.** 18 **21.** Multiplication
22. Addition **23.** $n - 2$ **24.** $n - k$ **25.** $15 + \frac{1}{2}n$
26. $m + 8$ **27.** $2n - 7$

Chapter 2 The Rules of Algebra

2•1 Recognizing Like Terms and Unlike Terms

1. $6y$ **3.** $15hp$ **5.** 2 **7.** 3 **9.** $5x, 6y$ **11.** Unlike
13. Unlike **15.** Yes **17.** No **19.** 30, 18, 9

2•2 Understanding the Properties of Numbers

1. 9 **3.** 9
5. Commutative Property of Multiplication
7. Associative Property of Addition
9. Associative Property of Multiplication

2•3 Understanding the Distributive Property of Multiplication Over Addition

1. 6 and 9 **3.** $8, x$ **5.** 3 **7.** $3 • 9 + 3 • 4$
9. $8a + 8b$ **11.** $4(x + y)$ **13.** 1,428

2•4   Adding Like Terms

1. Yes   3. Yes   5. No   7. $9p$
9. $9n$ 11. $16c + 11$ 13. $14k + 3n + 37$
15. a. $12m + 9n$; $15m + 7n$ b. $27m + 16n$

2•5   Subtracting Like Terms

1. No   3. Yes   5. Yes   7. $4g$ 9. $15w$ 11. $4.9a$
13. $4k$ 15. $17h^2 + 25h + 9$ 17. $7x^2$

2•6   Multiplying Terms

1. Yes   3. No   5. No   7. $28ab$ 9. $36mn$ 11. $20k^2$
13. $3c^2$ 15. $21st^2$ 17. $30h$ 19. $14c$ 21. $45c^2$

2•7   Dividing Terms

1. $\frac{24}{6}$ or $\frac{8}{2}$ 3. $\frac{x}{y}$ 5. $\frac{12n^2}{2n}$ 7. $6h$ 9. $12k$
11. c 13. $2a$ 15. $5m$ 17. $6c$

Chapter 2 Review

1. Distributive Property of Multiplication Over Addition
2. coefficient   3. factors
4. Terms: $2x, 3y, 5z$; coefficients: 2, 3, 5
5. Terms: $4m^3, 7m^2, 9.2m, 16$; coefficients: 4, 7, 9.2, 16
6. Unlike   7. Like   8. Like   9. Unlike   10. $20k$
    11. $9x$
12. $2n$ 13. $9h$ 14. $35e$ 15. $7a + 5b$ 16. $8n + 3m$
17. $6p$ 18. $10y^2$ 19. $6p^2$ 20. $9ab + 4a + 13$
21. $10x^2y + 8x + y$ 22. $40ac$ 23. $3d^2v^2$ 24. $30m^2n$
25. $5b$ 26. $8xz$ 27. 1   28. $16n, 8n, 48n^2, 3$
29. Identity Property of Addition
30. Commutative Property of Multiplication
31. Associative Property of Addition
32. Commutative Property of Addition
33. $6x + 6y$ 34. $6a^2 + 8ab + 10ac$
35. a. $3d, 5d$ b. $8d$

Chapter 3   Equations and Formulas

3•1   What Is an Equation?

1. Yes; $4(5) = 20$ 3. Open   5. True   7. 4
9. 3   11. 11   13. 0   15. 3.5   17. 4

3•2   Subtracting to Solve Equations

1. Subtract 5 from both sides.
3. Subtract 8 from both sides.
5. Subtract 13.7 from both sides.
7. 3   9. 3.5   11. 432

3•3   Adding to Solve Equations

1. Add 3 to both sides.
3. Add 5 to both sides.
5. 18   7. 8.3   9. 388

3•4   Dividing to Solve Equations

1. Dominick divided both sides by 8. Yes, he is correct.
3. Divide both sides by 7.
5. Divide both sides by 12.
7. 4   9. 6   11. 12   13. 1.5   15. 3.6
17. $\frac{4}{3}$ 19. 2   21. $\frac{1}{15}$ 23. 36   25. 18.4
27. a. $\frac{2}{3}s = 7.6$ b. 11.4 miles per hour

3•5 Multiplying to Solve Equations

1. Multiply both sides by 3.
3. Multiply both sides by 3.1.
5. Multiply both sides by 2.
7. 45 9. 84 11. 18 13. 48 15. 136
17. 23.7 19. 21 21. 40 23. 6
25. a. $4 = \frac{v}{25}$ b. 100 volts

3•6 What Is a Formula?

1. $20 = l(2)$ 3. $34 = (2)(12) + 2w$
5. $96 = 1.8C + 32$ 7. $26 = r - 5;$ 31
9. $A = (2.5)(1.8);$ 4.5 11. $12 = (\frac{1}{2})(8)h;$ 3

3•7 Solving Equations With Fractions and Mixed Numbers

1. Multiply by $\frac{6}{5}$, the multiplicative inverse of $\frac{5}{6}$.
3. Multiply by 7. 5. Multiply by $\frac{3}{5}$. 7. $67\frac{1}{2}$ 9. $3\frac{7}{12}$

Chapter 3 Review

1. equation 2. algebraic sentence
3. multiplicative inverse 4. proportion; ratios
5. solution 6. Open 7. False 8. True 9. Open
10. 16 11. 24 12. 35 13. 8 14. 64 15. 6
16. 21.75 17. Subtraction 18. Division 19. $\frac{8}{3}$
20. $\frac{1}{24}$ 21. 60 22. 153 23. $4\frac{1}{2}$
24. Possible answers: $\frac{1.5}{5} = \frac{m}{2.5}$; $\frac{3}{4}$ cup of milk; $\frac{3}{5} = \frac{f}{2.5}$; $1\frac{1}{2}$ cups of flour

Chapter 4   Integers

4•1 What Is an Integer?

1. The quarterback lost 4 yards.
3. The price of CDs went down $1.50.
5. Len spent $200 during April.
7. 6 9. -15 11. -20
13. Possible answers: Temperatures, or changes in temperature; account balances, or changes in account balances; yards gained or lost in football
15. 1,400; Possible answer: A positive integer because the point is above sea level

4•2 Integers and the Number Line

1. Yes. Positive 3 is three units to the right of zero and negative 2 is two units to the left of zero.
3. -7 5. 9 7. -9 9. F 11. Z 13. P

14–17.

4•3 Absolute Value

1. Yes. If a number is negative, its absolute value equals its opposite, which is a positive number.
3. 3 5. 0 7. 10 9. 5 11. $4\frac{1}{2}$ 13. 2.7 15. 5
17. 9 19. 63 21. 22°F

4•4 Which Integer Is Greater?

1. San Diego, Miami, Philadelphia, Atlanta. Found the percentage for each city on the number line, then listed the cities from right to left.
3. 7 5. -3 7. $<$ 9. $>$ 11. $<$ 13. $=$
15. $-8, 5, 7$ 17. $-2, -1, 0, 1$ 19. $-23, -20, -14, 14$
21. $-5 < 4$ and $4 > -5$

4•5　Adding Integers

1. 2

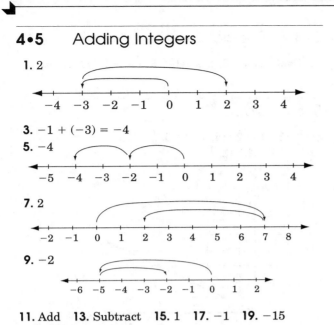

3. $-1 + (-3) = -4$

5. -4

7. 2

9. -2

11. Add　**13.** Subtract　**15.** 1　**17.** -1　**19.** -15
21. -4　**23.** 7　**25.** -12　**27.** -1

4•6　Subtracting Integers

1. $6 + (-10)$　**3.** $8 + 2$　**5.** -3　**7.** -11
9. -15　**11.** -25　**13.** -100　**15.** 3
17. -2　**19.** Profit; $1,450

4•7　Multiplying Integers

1. Negative　**3.** Positive　**5.** -18　**7.** 63　**9.** 80
11. -480　**13.** -8　**15.** -120　**17.** -4 and -5

4•8　Dividing Integers

1. Negative　**3.** Negative　**5.** -5　**7.** 2　**9.** 3
11. 6　**13.** -5　**15.** 14　**17.** 3　**19.** -30
21. a. $-18°F$　**b.** $-3°F$

Chapter 4 Review

1. g　**2.** b　**3.** h　**4.** a　**5.** d　**6.** c　**7.** f　**8.** e　**9.** 23
10. 0　**11.** -3　**12.** 2　**13.** 5　**14.** 9　**15.** 17.8　**16.** 7
17–19.

20. $-6, -3, 3, 6$　**21.** $-8, -5, -2, -1, 0, 1$　**22.** 2
23. -17　**24.** 7　**25.** -72　**26.** -11　**27.** 17　**28.** 400
29. -7　**30.** -4　**31.** -5　**32.** $=$　**33.** $<$　**34.** $>$　**35.** $>$
36. -12 ft　**37.** $-20¢$

Chapter 5　Introduction to Graphing

5•1　The Coordinate Plane

1. 2 west, 4 south　**3.** 3 west, 0 north or south
5–8.

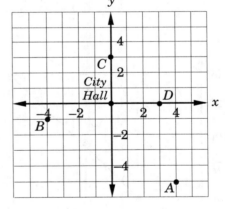

9. NW　**11.** NE　**13.** 9 blocks

5•2   Ordered Pairs

1. (4, 1)   3. (3, −4)   5. (−3, 4)

6–11.

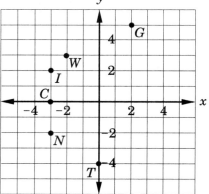

13. IV   15. 4   17. (6, −5)

5•3   Tables and Graphs

1. 7   3. −2

5.

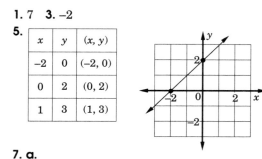

x	y	(x, y)
−2	0	(−2, 0)
0	2	(0, 2)
1	3	(1, 3)

7. a.

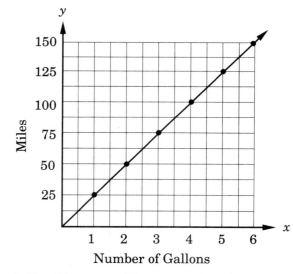

b. Possible answer: The car gets 25 miles per gallon.

5•4   Special Graphs

1. Continuous   3. Discrete   5. $x = -3$ 7. Discrete

5•5   Slope

1. $\frac{3}{2}$ 3. (1, −2); (4, 1); 1   5. $\frac{1}{2}$ 7. 9
9. 3   11. $-\frac{4}{7}$ 13. $\frac{1}{2}$

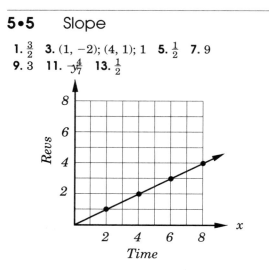

5•6   Finding the Intercepts of an Equation

1. 5; 3   3. −4; −1   5. 3; −6   7. $\frac{8}{5}$; −8
9. 5; 7   11. −40
13. a. 32°F   b. 40°C   c. slope: $\frac{9}{5}$; y-intercept: 32

Chapter 5 Review

1. axes   2. continuous line   3. coordinate plane
4. coordinates   5. graph of an equation
6. linear equation   7. origin   8. 14   9. 15
10. (−3, −4)   11. (3, 2)   12. (0, −1)
13–15.

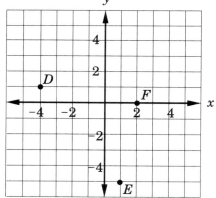

16. IV **17.** III **18.** 7 **19.** 25 **20.** −1 **21.** 18.5
22.

x	y	(x, y)
−1	−4	(−1, −4)
1	0	(1, 0)
3	4	(3, 4)

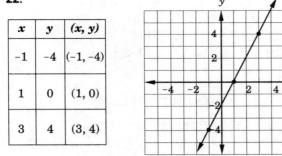

23. $x = 6$ **24.** −3 **25.** 2 **26.** $\frac{1}{4}$ **27.** 6; −6 **28.** 7; −4
29. 12 ft

Chapter 6 More About Graphing

6•1 Slope as Rate of Change

1. 0.03 **3.** −3 **5.** + 9¢

6•2 Using the Slope-Intercept Form of an Equation

1. Slope: −2; y-intercept: −5
3. Slope: $-\frac{2}{3}$; y-intercept: 4 **5.** $y = 4x − 1$
7. $y = \frac{2}{3}x − 1$

6•3 Other Forms of Equations

1. $-5x + 3y = 10$ **3.** $4x − 9y = 7$ **5.** $4x − 10y = −2$
7. $y = \frac{1}{2}x + 2$; student graph **9.** $48 = 6x + 8y$

6•4 Graphing Absolute-Value Equations

1. $y = 8$ **3.** $y = 3$
5. $x = −6$ $y = 2$
    $x = −5$ $y = 1$
    $x = −4$ $y = 0$
    $x = −3$ $y = 1$
    $x = −2$ $y = 2$
7. Possible answers: $x = −2, −1, 0, 1, 2$
    $y = 3, 2\frac{1}{2}, 2, 1\frac{1}{2}, 1$; student graph

6•5 Other Graphs and Their Equations

1. perpendicular. **3.** perpendicular **5.** 4 **7.** 6
9. $x = 0$ $y = 0$
    $x = 2$ $y = 6.4$
    $x = 4$ $y = 9.6$
    $x = 5$ $y = 10$
    $x = 6$ $y = 9.6$
    $x = 8$ $y = 6.4$
    $x = 10$ $y = 0$; student graph

Chapter 6 Review

1. perpendicular **2.** quadratic **3.** y-intercept form
4. $\frac{3}{−3} = −1$ **5.** $\frac{−8}{−2} = 4$ **6.** $y = 3x − 2$
7. $y = -\frac{3}{4}x + 4$ **8.** Slope: 1; y-intercept: 1
9. Slope: 4; y-intercept: 2 **10.** Slope: −2; y-intercept: 5
11. Slope: $\frac{1}{2}$; y-intercept: $\frac{3}{2}$ **12.** $4x − 3y = 1$
13. $2x + 6y = 8$ **14.** −5 **15.** $\frac{−5}{2}$
16. Possible answers: $x = −2, −1, 0, 1, 2$
    $y = 3, 2, 1, 0, 1$
17. Possible answers: $x = −2, −1, 0, 1, 2$
    $y = −2, −5, −6, −5, −2$
18. $\frac{−377}{23}$ **19.** $\frac{12}{5}$

Chapter 7 Exponents

7•1 More About Exponents

1. 6^4 3. 2^7 5. $3 \cdot 3 \cdot 3 \cdot 3 \cdot 3$
7. $9 \cdot 9$ 9. $x \cdot x \cdot x \cdot x \cdot x \cdot x$
11. 11   13. 125   15. 64   17. 2,097,152
19. No. $3^2 = 9$ and $2^3 = 8$, so they are not equal.

7•2 Writing Very Large and Very Small Numbers

1. No; 45.6 is not between 1 and 10.   3. No
5. Yes   7. No   9. 6; 10^6 11. $7 \cdot 10^6$ 13. $5.307 \cdot 10^4$
15. $8.8008 \cdot 10^{10}$ 17. 935,600   19. 3,070
21. $3.4 \cdot 10^8$ The number will be larger if the exponent is positive rather than negative.
23. $9.32 \cdot 10^{-4}$ 25. $5.810 \cdot 10^{-6}$ 27. $5.206 \cdot 10^{-3}$
29. 0.007064   31. 0.000001005   33. $\$4.09 \cdot 10^{50}$

7•3 Multiplication Properties of Exponents

1. 6^7 3. 9^7 5. 2^{21} 7. $125k^3$ 9. a^{11} 11. x^4y^6
13. a. 2^4p b. 16

7•4 Division Properties of Exponents

1. 3^5 3. 5^2 or 25   5. 10^4 or 10,000   7. $\frac{1}{32}$ 9. $\frac{a^3}{64}$
11. $2x^4$ 13. 2^2, or 4

7•5 Negative Exponents

1. $\frac{1}{8}$ 3. $\frac{1}{25}$ 5. $\frac{1}{128}$ 7. 1   9. $\frac{1}{144}$
11. $2^{-8} = \frac{1}{2^8}$ 13. $k^{-5} = \frac{1}{k^5}$ 15. $b^{-5} = \frac{1}{b^5}$
17. $-2m^{-2} = \frac{-2}{m^2}$ 19. $\frac{1}{12z^{-4}}$ 21. $3x^7y^2$

7•6 The Exponent of Zero

1. 1   3. 1   5. 1   7. $5^0 = 1$ 9. 3   11. $4a$
13. $8h^4k^3$ 15. 8, 4, 2, 1, $\frac{1}{2}$, $\frac{1}{4}$, $\frac{1}{8}$, $\frac{1}{16}$ 17. $\frac{1}{3}$ or $-\frac{1}{3}$

7•7 Radicals

1. Yes. Possible answer: Since x^2 cubed is $(x^2)^3 = x^6$, the cube root of x^6 is x^2.
3. $5x^3$ 5. -4 7. 10   9. 1   11. $-\frac{7}{10}$ 13. True
15. 3.2   17. 1.4   19. 9.2   21. 4.24   23. 10 in.
25. 127.28 ft   27. 47.4 sec

Chapter 7 Review

1. square   2. perfect square   3. radical
4. power or exponent   5. 9^4 6. b^3 7. 32
8. 100,000   9. $6.45 \cdot 10^4$ 10. $9 \cdot 10^{-4}$
11. $3.31 \cdot 10^{-7}$ 12. $1 \cdot 10^{11}$ 13. 0.05   14. 999
15. 0.0000010302   16. 81,100,000   17. 7^8 18. k^{10}
19. $27n^3$ 20. $2^{20}p^{18}$ 21. $\frac{1}{8}$ 22. $\frac{1}{6^4}$ 23. $\frac{1}{5}$ 24. $\frac{c^4}{7^4}$
25. $2x^6$ 26. 27   27. 9   28. $\frac{\sqrt{3}}{8}$ 29. $-7x^4$ 30. $\frac{4}{5}$
31. 1.1 sec   32. 50 mi/h

Chapter 8   Inequalities

8•1   Equations and Inequalities

1. $x < 4$ 3. $x \le -1$
5.

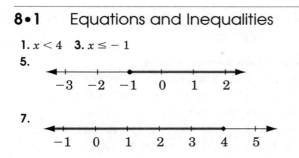

7.

9. $x < 5$ 11. $x \le 3$ 13. $4,600

8•2   Solving One-Step Inequalities

1. Should be reversed   3. Stays the same
5. $x < -6$ 7. $x < -5$ 9. $n > 52$
11. a. $l - 0.03 \le l \le l + 0.03$ b. 10.7 cm

8•3   Solving Two-Step Inequalities

1. Subtract 4.   3. Subtract 5.   5. $x \ge 4$ 7. $x \ge 78$
9. $x > 48$ 11. $x \ge 7$
13. a. $300 + 40h \le 1,600$ b. $32.5\ h$

Chapter 8 Review

1. inequality   2. Tolerance   3. budget   4. $x \ge 2$
5. $x < 5$ 6. $x > -2$ 7. $x \le -3$
8.

9.

10.

11.

12. Stays the same   13. Stays the same
14. Should be reversed   15. Should be reversed
16. Divide by 5.   17. Multiply by -6.   18. Add 6.
19. Subtract 14.   20. $x > 4$ 21. $p \le 17$ 22. $k > -20$
23. $x \ge -15$ 24. $c < 6$ 25. $x \le -27$ 26. $x > 10$
27. $p > 3$ 28. $h \le 48$
29. a. $n \le 50$, $n > 50$, and $n \le 100$ b. $457.50

Chapter 9   Monomials and Polynomials

9•1   Recognizing Monomials and Polynomials

1. trinomial   3. binomial   5. 4   7. 3   9. 4
11. 5   13. $3b, 7b, 4b$ 15. $2ac^2, 9ac^2$

9•2   Adding and Subtracting Polynomials

1. $5n + 1$ 3. $22ab$ 5. $2x^2 - 2x + 16$
7. $-x^2 + 6x - 9$ 9. $2x^3 + 5y^2 + 27$ cubic units

9•3   Multiplying a Polynomial by a Monomial

1. $27rw$ 3. $14x^3$ 5. $24a^2b + 20ab^2$
7. $40x^3 - 40x^2 - 64x$ 9. $7a^3 + 56a^2$
11. $8x^3 + 12x^2 - 24x$ 13. $-9st^2 - 9st + 81$
15. $12k^2 - 12k + 36$
17. Jacob's intermediate step was correct as
$30x^5 + 42x^4 + 12x^3$. This is the final answer.
Jacob's mistake is adding unlike terms together.
You cannot add terms in x^5, x^4, x^3 together to get a
single term in x^{12}.
19. $10a^3bc + 15ab^3c + 20abc^3$
21. $-2x^3y^3z^3 - 2x^3y^3z^2 - 2x^3y^3z^2 = -2x^3y^3z^3 - 4x^3y^3z^2$
23. $92(w^2 + 15w)$

9•4 Multiplying Polynomials

1. $n^3 - n^2 + n - 6$
3. $n^2 + n - 20$
5. $10x^2 + x - 24$
7. $2n^3 - 13n^2 + 22n - 8$
9. $3x^3 - 13x^2 - 46x - 24$
11. $2x^4 + 5x^3 - 13x^2 + 19x - 28$
13. $x^2 + 16x + 63$
15. $x^2 - 7x - 18$
17. $2x^2 + 7x + 6$
19. $28x^2 + 13x - 63$
21. $(3x + 4)(x + 4) = 3x^2 + 16x + 16$ in.^{2}

Chapter 9 Review

1. c 2. e 3. d 4. a 5. b 6. trinomial; 3
7. monomial; 9 8. binomial; 1 9. trinomial; 2
10. $11j - 2$ 11. $3x^2 - 9$ 12. $7w + 8$
13. $x^3 + 3x^2 + 12x$ 14. $2a^2 + 3ac$ 15. $-2d + 2$
16. $32bc$ 17. $4n^3 + 12n^2 - 28n$
18. $6a^2b^2c + 8a^2b^3c + 10ab^2c^2$
19. $x^2 + 12x + 32$ 20. $6x^2 - 13x - 28$
21. $4x^4 + 12x^3 + x^2 - 22x - 15$
22. Each shelf area = 18 in. • 36 in. = 648 in.^{2}. Each cupboard has 2 shelves and she has 6 cupboards. Total shelf area = 6 • 2 • 648 in.^{2} = 7,776 in.^{2}. One roll of shelf paper covers 1,000 in.^{2}. Tina must buy 8 rolls of shelf paper.
23. 269 in.^{2}
24. 165,248 in.^{3}; 165,248 peanuts

Chapter 10 Factoring

10•1 Finding the Greatest Common Factor

1. Yes; 7 divides evenly into 84.
3. 45: 1, 3, 5, 9, 15, 45; 65: 1, 5, 13, 65; GCF is 5
5. 80: 1, 2, 4, 5, 8, 10, 16, 20, 40, 80; 104: 1, 2, 4, 8, 13, 26, 52, 104; GCF is 8
7. 18: 1, 2, 3, 6, 9, 18; 36: 1, 2, 3, 4, 6, 9, 12, 18, 36; 72: 1, 2, 3, 4, 6, 9, 12, 18, 36, 72; GCF is 18
9. 8: 1, 2, 4, 8; 15: 1, 3, 5, 15; 49: 1, 7, 49; GCF is 1
11. $6b$ 13. $2xy$ 15. $8rs$ 17. $1t^2v$ 19. 1
21. Possible answers: $6a^3b^2$, $12a^5b^3$, $18a^4b^3$
23. 15

10•2 Factoring Expressions

1. Work backwards and multiply each term
3. $5p^2$ 5. 1 7. $3x$ 9. $2a^2b^2(7a^2 + 8b)$
11. $3c^3d^6(3c^2 + 4d)$ 13. $2mn(2mn - 3)$
15. $(p - 5)(p - 3)$ 17. $(w - 6)(w + 5)$
19. $(x - 4)(x - 3)$ 21. $4b^2 + 24b + 32$

10•3 Factoring Quadratic Expressions

1. Yes. Each quantity has a common factor of 2.
3. $(7a + 1)(a + 2)$ 5. $(x - 1)(2x - 9)$
7. $(2a + 3)(a - 2)$ 9. $(11a + 4)(a - 5)$
11. $5(q + 5)(q + 2)$ 13. $6(p + 1)(p + 1)$
15. $8(x + 2)(x - 1)$ 17. $(3w + 4)(2w - 1)$
19. $2(4k - 1)(k - 1)$ 21. $(x^2 + 6x)(x - 2)$
23. a. $(3x - 2)$ and $(x + 4)$ b. 4 ft $\times$ 8 ft $\times$ 10 ft

10•4 Factoring Differences of Two Squares and Perfect Square Trinomials

1. Yes. Both terms are perfect squares
3. $(5r + 6)(5r - 6)$ 5. $(x^2 + 7)(x^2 - 7)$
7. $(2a^2 - 3b)(2a^2 + 3b)$ 9. $(a^4 + b^2)(a^4 - b^2)$
11. $(8 - w^2v)(8 + w^2v)$
13. $(x - 5)^2$ 15. $(m - 6)^2$
17. not a perfect square trinomial
19. a. $4x^2 + 60x + 225$ b. perfect square trinomial

10•5 Zero Products

1. $x = -5$ or $x = 5$ 3. $v = -5$ or $v = -6$
5. $z = -14$ or $z = -21$ 7. $n = 19$ or $n = 117$
9. $w = 0$ or $w = -1$ 11. $(x + 8)(x - 6) = 0$

10•6 Solving Equations by Factoring

1. Subtract 21 from both sides.
3. $n = -6$ or $n = -4$ 5. $x = \frac{3}{5}$ or $x = -1$
7. $x = \frac{5}{2}$ or $x = -2$ 9. $w = \frac{3}{5}$ or $w = 2$
11. $x = 0$ or $x = 3$ or $x = 4$
13. $y = 0$ or $y = 2$ or $y = -2$
15. $w^2 - 3w - 108 = 0$. The lower bed cannot have a negative $w = -12$ or $w = 9$ dimension. So the width is 9 and the length is 12 ft.

10•7 The Quadratic Formula

1. $x \approx 1.22$ or -0.55 3. $r = -0.5$ or -2
5. $x \approx 0.17$ or 5.93
7. **a.** $n^2 + (n + 1)^2 = (n + 2)^2$ **b.** $n = 3$ or -1

Chapter 10 Review

1. greatest common factor
2. quadratic formula
3. differences of two squares
4. 3   5. 1   6. 4   7. $3x$ 8. $3a^3b^2(6ba - 4)$
9. $(x + 1)(x - 9)$ 10. $(b - 9)(b + 9)$
11. $2(2y - 1)(y + 2)$ 12. $(3r - 5)(3r + 2)$
13. $(4x + 5)(4x + 5)$ 14. $(y - 7)(y + 6)$
15. $(3a - 2b)(3a + 2b)$ 16. $t = -3$ or $t = -1$
17. $x = 0$ or $x = 8$ 18. $m = -15$ or $m = 17$
19. $n = 0$ or $n = 2$ or $n = 3$ 20. $w = 1$ or $w = 11$
21. $x = 5$ or $x = -4$ 22. $r = \frac{5}{2}$ or $r = -7$
23. $y = -\frac{3}{5}$ or $y = 2$ 24. $r \approx 3.58$ or 0.42
25. $x \approx -0.76$ or -5.24 26. $m \approx 0.56$ or -3.56
27. $x \approx 0.39$ or -3.9 28. 11 inches by 17 inches

Chapter 11 Systems of Equations

11•1 What Is a System of Equations?

1. No   3. Yes   5. Yes   7. $y = x + 4$, $x + y = 36$

11•2 Solving a System of Equations by Graphing

1. Possible answer: $(1, 8)$; $(2, 9)$; $(3, 10)$
3. $(1, -1)$;

x	y		x	y
0	−2		0	1
1	−1		1	−1
2	0		2	−3

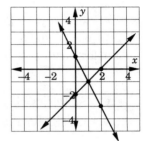

5. $(-2, 1)$;

x	y		x	y
0	0		0	3
2	−1		1	4
4	−2		2	5

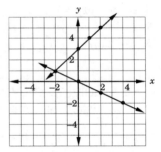

7. no solution;

x	y		x	y
0	0		0	$\frac{1}{3}$
1	2		1	$2\frac{1}{3}$
2	4		2	$4\frac{1}{3}$

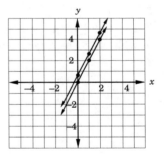

9. 2 hours later

11•3 Solving a System of Equations Using Addition or Subtraction

1. No. Possible answer: Wanda solved correctly for x, but then she solved incorrectly for y, which should be −2.
3. $x = 2$ and $y = 4$ 5. $x = \frac{9}{2}$ and $y = \frac{15}{8}$
7. Possible answer: Rearrange the terms in the system of equations. Then use either the addition method (if rearranged to $-x - 4y = -3$ and $x + 3y = 9$) or the subtraction method (if rearranged to $x + 4y = 3$ and $x + 3y = -9$).
9. $x = \frac{1}{5}$ and $y = -\frac{3}{5}$ 11. $x = 3$ and $y = -1$
13. $2x + y = 58$ and $6x + y\ 118$; $15 for T-shirts and $28 for jeans

11•4 Solving a System of Equations Using Multiplication

1. $x = 9$ and $y = 6$ 3. $x = 27$ and $y = 10$
5. $x = 6$ and $y = 5$ 7. first by 2; second by 3
9. $x = -\frac{22}{13}$ and $y = \frac{29}{13}$ 11. $x = -\frac{3}{11}$ and $y = \frac{64}{11}$
13. $x = 2$ and $y = 5$

11•5 Solving a System of Equations Using Substitution

1. Possible answer: Replace the y in the second equation with $4x$.
3. $x = 4$ and $y = -2$ 5. $x = 2$ and $y = 4$
7. $x = 1$ and $y = 7$ 9. $x = -3$, $y = -5\frac{1}{2}$
11. width is 80 feet; length is 240 feet

Chapter 11 Review

1. system of equations   2. Solution set
3. graphing; addition or subtraction with multiplication; substitution
4. Yes   5. Yes   6. No   7. Yes
8. (2, 3)

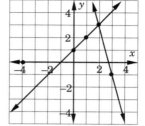

9. (1, 4)

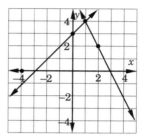

10. $x = \frac{5}{3}$ and $y = \frac{10}{3}$ 11. $x = \frac{5}{2}$ and $y = 2$
12. $x = 6$ and $y = 7$ 13. $x = -\frac{102}{29}$ and $y = -\frac{50}{29}$
14. $x = 12$ and $y = 8$ 15. $x = -\frac{22}{13}$ and $y = \frac{29}{13}$
16. 4 and 8
17. plants are $2; seeds are $1
18. 10 quarters
19. Robin has 15 CDs; Nigel has 33 CDs